LOVE FORTY

This play was first produced by Grassroots Productions at The Sherman Theatre, Cardiff, on the 16th September 1995, with the following cast of characters:

Marcia	Menna Trussler
Ralph	Gareth Morris
Girl Marcia	Helen Griffin
Boy Ralph	Ian Jeffs

Directed by Phil Clark

Love Forty

A play

Frank Vickery

Samuel French — London
New York - Toronto - Hollywood

CHARACTERS

Marcia
Ralph
Girl Marcia
Boy Ralph

The action of the play takes place in the bedroom of a detached house that was built sometime during the early fifties

ACT I Friday. 7.00 p.m.

ACT II The same night. 8.00 p.m.

Time—between 1955 and 1995

Other plays by Frank Vickery
published by Samuel French Ltd

Full length:
All's Fair
Biting the Bullet
Breaking the String
Easy Terms
Erogenous Zones
Family Planning
A Kiss on the Bottom
Loose Ends
A Night on the Tiles
One O'Clock from the House
Roots and Wings
Spanish Lies
Trivial Pursuits

One act:
After I'm Gone
Green Favours
A Night Out
Split Ends

ACT I

A bedroom of a detached house. Friday, 7 p.m.

The room is the master bedroom of the house and should not reflect any particular style or period. The choice of furniture and fittings should create an ambiguity which will allow the story to move from one time scale to another without questions

The room has wardrobes, a double bed with cabinets either side, a dressing-table (with an imaginary mirror) and stool, a rather large heavily upholstered bedroom chair, an ali-baba basket, and an exercise bike. There are two doors. One leads to the en-suite bathroom, the other out on to the landing and other rooms

When the Lights come up there is no-one on stage. Opening music from the auditorium suddenly comes out of the stereo which is on a low table at the foot of the bed

After a short time Marcia comes out of the bathroom, closing the door behind her. She has a towel wrapped around her head. She is wearing a dressing-gown. She also has a small towel around her neck. As she enters the room she removes the neck towel and disposes of it in the ali-baba basket which is against the wall just behind the exercise bike. She comes to sit at the dressing-table. She rummages idly through her make-up. It is while she is doing this that she eventually looks up and out, obviously pre-occupied with something

Suddenly Ralph is heard calling off

Ralph (*off*) Marcia?

She is motionless

(*Off*) Marcy, where are you? (*Calling again*) Marcy?

She snaps herself out of her deep thought

Marcia (*calling*) Yes?

She gets up and switches off the stereo, then returns to the dressing-table. A second or two passes

There is a sound effect, maybe of a few piano notes, middle scale, ending on a low note, and the Lights change to a bluish wash as a young Marcia tentatively enters the bedroom from the landing. She is dressed in a two-piece suit of the fifties period. She is carrying a handbag and wearing a corsage. She is dressed all in grey and wearing light grey make-up. She and young Ralph will keep this look throughout the play. She is obviously very impressed with the room. She even giggles to herself as she crosses to the back and moves towards the bed. She sits on it, tentatively, trying it out

Suddenly there is another call for Marcia from outside the room

Boy Ralph (*off*) Marcia?
Girl Marcia In here.

She hurries from the bed and sits next to Marcia at the dressing-table

Boy Ralph appears just inside the door. As he does so there is a sound effect

Boy Ralph Can I come in?
Girl Marcia Why not? It's your bedroom too, isn't it?

A young Ralph steps further into the room wearing clothes of the same period and colour as Girl Marcia

Boy Ralph Well, what do you think?
Girl Marcia About what?
Boy Ralph The house ... the bedroom.
Girl Marcia Oh, it's very nice, Ralph ... it really is.
Boy Ralph And we can have it for as long as we like ... well, within reason. And if they don't transfer my manager back, who knows, we might even have first refusal to buy it.
Girl Marcia Can you afford something like this?
Boy Ralph I can if I stay in the bank. We get favourable rates.
Girl Marcia I can't imagine me living here. You ... I see you, but not me.
Boy Ralph We've only been married a couple of hours ... not having second thoughts already, are you?
Girl Marcia Of course not. I didn't mean that, I just meant ——
Boy Ralph (*affectionately*) I know what you meant. (*Slight pause as he sits on the arm of the chair*) How are you feeling?
Girl Marcia Truthfully?
Boy Ralph (*trying to laugh*) No ... lie to me. I think you'd better lie.
Girl Marcia (*after a slight pause*) I'm confused.
Boy Ralph That's the truth, isn't it?
Girl Marcia Things are complicated enough as it is ... let's not make it worse by lying. We did promise always to be truthful with each other.

Boy Ralph Yes we did.
Girl Marcia So let's stick to it.
Marcia Things were simpler then.
Ralph (*off*) What was that?
Boy Ralph Tell me what's confusing you.
Girl Marcia Perhaps confused is the wrong word. Worried is a better one.
Boy Ralph What do they say, "A worry shared is a worry halved"?
Girl Marcia Not in our case ... and I think it's "Problem".
Boy Ralph Sorry?
Girl Marcia It's a problem shared, et cetera.
Marcia Silly sod.
Ralph (*off*) You talking to me?
Boy Ralph Problem, worry ... it's all the same.
Girl Marcia If you're honest you're just as worried as I am.
Boy Ralph About what?
Girl Marcia Us ... about what we've done. What people will say.
Boy Ralph What we've done is our business ... just remember I'll always do my best for you.
Girl Marcia But the fact that we don't love each other ——
Boy Ralph Means we can't get hurt ... and if no-one gets hurt, where's the harm in it?
Marcia Yes, much simpler then.
Ralph (*off*) I'm just popping downstairs.
Girl Marcia (*after a slight pause*) Do you think we should have told Clive and Barbara?
Boy Ralph About what?
Girl Marcia How we feel.
Boy Ralph No. They were only our witnesses. What's it to do with them? What's it to do with anyone?
Girl Marcia No regrets then?
Boy Ralph None. You?
Marcia No, no ... you didn't ask me.
Girl Marcia No regrets then?
Boy Ralph None.
Marcia That's right ... and then I said ——
Girl Marcia What if things change? What if there's a knock on the door one day and it's ... what's her name?
Boy Ralph Who?
Girl Marcia } (*together*) Who indeed.
Marcia
Girl Marcia Your fiancée.
Boy Ralph Sheila? And it goes without saying she's my ex.
Girl Marcia What would happen then?

Boy Ralph It could just as easily be your Peter at the door.
Girl Marcia He's not *my* Peter, and I asked first.
Boy Ralph This is silly. We both know that's not going to happen.
Girl Marcia All right, forget Peter and Sheila.
Boy Ralph Yes.
Girl Marcia What if someone else comes along?
Boy Ralph Like who?
Girl Marcia Anyone.
Boy Ralph It's pointless worrying about it. That could happen to any couple whether they married on the re-bound or not.
Girl Marcia (*after a slight pause*) Did anyone tell you that you're making a big mistake?
Boy Ralph By marrying you?

She nods

Oh, lots. (*He smiles as he moves* L *of the dressing-table*) You?
Girl Marcia Hundreds. (*She giggles*) So it really doesn't bother you that we don't love each other?
Boy Ralph We like each other. Love might grow.
Girl Marcia And if it doesn't?
Boy Ralph It doesn't. (*He comes to sit on the dressing-table stool. Now they're sitting either side of Marcia*) Anyway the baby is bound to bring us together.

He stretches his hand along the table and Girl Marcia gently touches it

Girl Marcia (*after a slight pause*) I hope I'll never hurt you.
Boy Ralph It's only a piece of paper you know, this marriage.
Girl Marcia (*taking back her hand*) Oh, Ralph.
Boy Ralph Well, it is ... right now it is. It's the easiest thing in the world for either of us to get up and walk away.
Marcia That's right.
Girl Marcia But I don't want to walk away.
Boy Ralph Of course you don't ... and at the moment neither do I ... but we both know if ever we want to then it's OK.
Girl Marcia But what if it's not? What if in ten years' time——
Marcia Or forty ——
Girl Marcia — one of us wants to go and it's not all right with the other? What happens then?
Boy Ralph The secret is not to think that far ahead. We've made a pledge not to look any further than tomorrow ... with a bit of luck we might not only find we have a future together, slowly between us perhaps we can build a past.

Girl Marcia And if it doesn't work out ——
Boy Ralph We move on ... in different directions.
Girl Marcia Without looking back.
Marcia That's a laugh.
Girl Marcia (*after a slight pause*) What if we move on without moving out?
Boy Ralph Now we've gone full circle. I don't think we should make the rules beforehand. The way to do it is to create them as we go along ... that way they can be customized. Have the rules suit us and not us suit the rules.
Girl Marcia I see.
Marcia I must have been off my bloody head.
Boy Ralph You have to have doubts you know ... (*he gets up and stands behind Girl Marcia*) ... if only for me to re-assure you.
Girl Marcia And you? What do you have?
Boy Ralph Butterflies.

She laughs

I do. Let's try and always remember how it feels now ... the longer we're together the harder it's going to be to hang on to it.
Marcia You're not kidding.
Girl Marcia Perhaps we'll never be as excited together as we are tonight.
Boy Ralph In a way that's how it should be ... but we've got to remember how it is so we can use it as our yardstick.
Girl Marcia Should we measure things against this?
Boy Ralph Only to gauge how close we are at any given time.
Marcia Or how far apart.
Boy Ralph If we ever have doubts, and I'm sure we will, all we have to do is think back to now.
Girl Marcia That might not make us feel better.
Boy Ralph I didn't say it would ... it may help us see things more clearly, though.
Marcia Well you're right there.
Girl Marcia (*after a slight pause*) I could sit up all night talking.
Boy Ralph (*disappointed*) Really?
Girl Marcia I won't of course.
Boy Ralph You can if you want to. No pressure, remember.
Girl Marcia It's our wedding night.
Boy Ralph So what.
Girl Marcia Do *you* want to talk?
Boy Ralph Not really.
Girl Marcia (*after a slight pause*) Bed then.

A slight pause as all three look towards the bed

Girl Marcia (*spotting the bathroom door*) Oh, what's through there? (*She gets up and goes to it*)
Boy Ralph The en-suite. (*He follows her*)
Girl Marcia (*opening the door and briefly looking in*) Oh, very swish ... very posh.
Boy Ralph Everything's ready for you.
Girl Marcia Ready for me?
Boy Ralph Your little case ... your bits and bobs.
Girl Marcia Are you going to spoil me?
Boy Ralph I might.

They kiss

Marcia (*looking at them*) And for a while you did.
Ralph (*off, calling*) Marcy!
Girl Marcia (*looking back into the bathroom*) You didn't have to set it all out.
Boy Ralph I know.

Ralph comes into the room. He is carrying a bottle of champagne and two glasses

Ralph There you are ... why didn't you answer?
Girl Marcia Are you going to join me?
Marcia I did.

Ralph sets the bottle and glasses down on the low table at the foot of the bed. Marcia spots the Moët

Champagne?
Boy Ralph No, I'll use the other bathroom ... just for tonight.

Boy Ralph crosses upstage and goes out on to the landing. Girl Marcia turns and goes into the bathroom. The Lights change

Ralph Yes, champagne ... why not. It's a bit of a milestone after all.
Marcia Millstone.
Ralph (*laughing, opening the champagne*) Why do you say things like that, you know you don't mean them.
Marcia (*continuing to make-up*) Don't I?
Ralph Of course you don't. Who were you talking to?
Marcia What?
Ralph I heard you. Have you been on the phone?

Marcia No ... I've been thinking aloud, that's all.

Ralph Talking to yourself, eh? You know what they say about that.

Marcia I've heard you do it too.

Ralph Nonsense. I was going to keep this until you came downstairs (*meaning the champagne*), but I think we're running a bit late so best open it now.

Marcia There's plenty of time, we don't have to be there till half-seven.

Ralph Who told you that?

Marcia I don't know ... you, I suppose.

Ralph No, not guilty...

Marcia Perhaps it was Judith then.

Ralph Have you enjoyed your day?

Marcia It's been all right.

Ralph That says a lot.

Marcia No, it's been lovely ... really.

Ralph Lovely?

Marcia Yes.

Ralph I take you for lunch, we play a round of golf, I arrange delivery of forty red roses and all you can think of to come up with is, "lovely".

Marcia All right it was wonderful, then. Is that what you want to hear? Thank you, Ralph, for a wonderful day. You take me for a five-course lunch and I'm on a diet ——

Ralph I didn't know you were on a diet.

Marcia We play a round of golf — I don't play golf ——

Ralph How long have you been dieting?

Marcia Eight months ... and you send me flowers knowing I suffer from hay-fever.

Ralph Ah yes, I forgot about that.

Marcia At the risk of repeating myself I'll say it again, thank you, Ralph, I've truly had a wonderful day.

Ralph pops the champagne and proceeds to pour two glasses

Ralph Well, I did my best.

Marcia For forty years you've said you've done your best.

Ralph Well then.

Marcia Well then, what?

Ralph (*handing her a glass of champagne*) Well then ... Cheers!

They sip. Marcia returns to her make-up. Ralph just stands there rather awkwardly

I thought it was a very nice day.

Marcia Good.
Ralph After all, it is my day as well.
Marcia Of course it is.
Ralph People tend to forget that, don't they?
Marcia What?
Ralph That it's as much of an anniversary for the man as it is for the woman.
  I mean after all ... he's gone the course too.
Marcia Meaning you?
Ralph In this instance, yes. Don't you agree?
Marcia What? That it's as much of an occasion for the man as the woman?
  Or that people tend to forget as much?
Ralph Both, I suppose.
Marcia (*thinking about it*) Yes and yes.
Ralph Well, I've had a wonderful day, anyway.
Marcia I'm only thankful it's just a quiet meal with the girls.
Ralph (*after a slight pause*) Really?
Marcia The last thing I'd want tonight is to face a crowd.
Ralph You're not sorry they didn't arrange a huge surprise party then?
Marcia God, no. I don't think I could smile for three hours.
Ralph Drink up.

She reaches out to hand him her glass but he has taken it long before

Marcia (*after a slight pause*) Where are we eating tonight, I don't think you
  told me the name of the restaurant?
Ralph (*pouring*) Er ... Stephano's.
Marcia Is it new? I haven't heard of it.
Ralph It's very new.
Marcia Do you know anyone who's been there?
Ralph Not a soul.
Marcia Well it must be all right. The girls wouldn't have booked us in just
  anywhere.
Ralph (*after a slight pause; trying to laugh*) Do you know who I was thinking
  about the other day? Malcolm and Eileen ...
Marcia (*taking the towel from her head*) Who?
Ralph He used to work with me in the bank ... years ago. We all used to spend
  a lot of time together.
Marcia Is that so.
Ralph You and Eileen got on like a house on fire. (*He sets her glass back
  down on the dressing-table*)
Marcia Really?
Ralph You were very close.
Marcia Now that is frightening.

Ralph Why?

Marcia Because I don't know who the hell you're talking about.

Ralph We were all very close. We still get a Christmas card every year. It's always the one with a poinsettia on the front.

Marcia I remember the card.

Ralph I'd love to see them again.

Marcia Get in touch then.

Ralph Yes. I've got an address. Wouldn't you like to see them again?

Marcia I might if I could remember who the hell they were.

Ralph The times we all had dinner together.

Marcia Where?

Ralph Our house and theirs ...

Marcia And when was all this?

Ralph Oh, twenty-five years ago at least.

Marcia For some reason I've completely blanked them out.

Ralph She was a real character.

Marcia What was her name again?

Ralph Eileen.

Marcia Eileen. And his?

Ralph Malcolm.

Marcia Malcolm. Nothing.

Ralph Do you remember Clive and Barbara?

Marcia What do you take me for? Of course I remember Clive and Barbara, they were witnesses at our wedding.

Ralph We haven't seen them for a while.

Marcia What is it with you?

Ralph What?

Marcia You seem to be thinking a lot about people you haven't seen lately.

Ralph Well you do. When you reach our age, you do.

Marcia *I* don't.

Ralph What do you think about then?

Marcia (*picking up her drink*) Largely about how I'm going to get through the day.

Ralph There you are ... (*He laughs*) You're doing it again.

Marcia What?

Ralph You're saying things you don't mean.

Marcia I do mean it.

Ralph I suppose it's your sense of humour.

Marcia I didn't say it to be funny.

Ralph What did you say it for then?

Marcia Because it's the truth.

Ralph That's one of the things I've always liked about you, your sense of humour.

Marcia (*firmly*) Ralph, I'm not trying to be funny!
Ralph You don't have to ... it just comes natural with you ... it always has.
Marcia Why don't you ever listen to me?
Ralph I do.
Marcia All right, what did I just say?
Ralph You said you're not trying to be funny.
Marcia That means you heard me, it doesn't mean you listened.
Ralph (*after a slight pause*) Ah, now you've foxed me there.
Marcia Just forget it.
Ralph Top you up?

Again, she reaches for her glass but he beats her to it

(*As he pours*) What about Kay and Benny?
Marcia What about them?
Ralph We haven't seen them since God knows when.
Marcia Now this may surprise you but they haven't seen us either.
Ralph Ah, that's sarcasm ... now that's not funny at all. (*He places her glass back down on the dressing-table*)
Marcia Is there something going on with you?
Ralph No! Of course not ... definitely not. What makes you think there's something going on?
Marcia Because you're beginning to play on my nerves.
Ralph (*moving* DR) Well, there's nothing. Nothing. We're going out for a nice quiet Chinese meal with the girls.
Marcia Chinese?
Ralph What's wrong?
Marcia Are you sure?
Ralph Of course I'm sure. What's wrong?
Marcia Well, nothing ... except I've never heard of a Chinese restaurant called Stephano's before.
Ralph Where on earth did you get Stephano's from?
Marcia You.
Ralph (*laughing*) No, I don't think so.
Marcia I'm telling you.
Ralph No, no ... we're definitely eating Chinese. (*He looks a little worried*)
Marcia I think it's time we both sat down and wrote our living wills.
Ralph What for?
Marcia I'm not sure who at this stage, but one of us is beginning to show definite signs of dementia. If it turns out to be me I want the pillow over my face.
Ralph Sorry, no can do.
Marcia Why not? I'd do the same for you.

Ralph Would you?

Marcia If it's what you wanted.

Ralph You mean you'd actually be capable of suffocating me?

Marcia I couldn't bear it if your brain all scrambled and you didn't know who the hell I was.

Ralph I don't think I know who the hell you are *now*. You'd actually put a pillow over my face and stop me breathing.

Marcia Yes ... if I thought I'd get away with it. I wouldn't go to prison for you.

Ralph (*smiling*) Forty years and you're still surprising me.

Marcia (*getting up and putting the second towel away in the basket*) Well, there you are, you see. Not everyone can say that.

Ralph (*sitting on the side of the bed*) Probably that's one of the reasons why we've lasted so long ... thank God there's still nooks and crannies we haven't discovered about each other.

Marcia (*returning to the side of the dressing-table and picking up her glass*) Oh, there's not much I don't know about you.

Ralph Are you saying you see through me?

Marcia Transparent as glass. (*She holds up her drink before sipping it*)

Ralph What if you're wrong? What if I've got some deep dark secret you don't know about?

Marcia Have you?

Ralph (*smiling*) Maybe.

Marcia No, I know everything about you. I even know about your fling.

Ralph (*after a slight pause*) What fling?

Marcia The one you had three years after we were married.

Ralph looks

We promised always to be truthful but we weren't ... well, at least *you* weren't.

Ralph Why are you bringing this up now?

Marcia I don't know. (*Slight pause*) I knew the first time you went out with her.

Ralph What?

Marcia We had a babysitter that night because I'd gone out too. I was home before you though.

Girl Marcia appears. The Lights change and there is a sound effect. She comes to sit at the dressing-table

I was sitting at the dressing-table taking off my make-up when you came in.

The bedroom door opens and Boy Ralph comes in. There is a sound effect

Boy Ralph Hallo.

Girl Marcia looks up and smiles

Marcia Don't ask me how but you looked different.
Girl Marcia You're late. Good time?
Boy Ralph Yes, fine.
Ralph I don't remember much about it.
Marcia It's incredible how much we throw out with the rubbish.
Girl Marcia Just fine?
Boy Ralph (*sitting in the chair*) No, I enjoyed myself. (*He takes off his tie*)
Girl Marcia Good.
Marcia (*crossing L to Boy Ralph*) You said something about having had a good time ——
Boy Ralph I had a good time ... in fact, the lads are talking about meeting up every week.
Girl Marcia That'll be nice.
Marcia I can see your face now as you set up your Friday nights.
Boy Ralph That's all right with you, is it?
Girl Marcia Yes, of course.
Marcia You looked so guilty.
Ralph And different you said.
Marcia Yes.
Ralph In what way?
Marcia (*moving around the back of the chair to face Ralph*) Difficult to say. There was a definite lack of eye contact.

Girl Marcia looks at Boy Ralph but he avoids her gaze

Ralph You actually remember that?
Marcia And an immediate change of subject.
Boy Ralph What sort of night have *you* had?
Girl Marcia Boring actually. It'll be a hell of a long time before I have another night out with the girls from the residents' committee.
Ralph I'm sorry.
Girl Marcia I just can't talk about knickers, shoes and bedwetting.
Marcia I remember you came over and caught hold of me.

Boy Ralph goes over, holds Girl Marcia from behind and starts kissing her neck

Ralph How can you go back all those years?

Marcia It was important. Our relationship was entering a new phase.
Boy Ralph Let's go to bed.
Marcia You wanted to have sex with me.
Girl Marcia What's the matter with you tonight?
Boy Ralph Come on.
Ralph It didn't mean anything ... you know, the other thing.
Marcia I reckoned you thought by having sex with me I'd be less suspicious
of you having had sex with someone else.

Girl Marcia pushes Boy Ralph away

Boy Ralph What?
Marcia I could smell her on you.
Girl Marcia Shower first.
Marcia For three months I was suspicious of anyone wearing, "Evening in
Paris".
Boy Ralph (*heading for the bathroom door*) Do you want to shower with
me?
Girl Marcia I'll be in in a minute.

Boy Ralph goes off

Ralph I didn't mean to hurt you.
Marcia You didn't hurt me ... you just threw me for a moment, that's all.
Suddenly someone knocked on that door we talked about and I wasn't sure
where our relationship would go from there. (*Slight pause*) I didn't want
to have sex with you that night; not because I didn't fancy it — to be honest,
knowing you'd just been with someone else was a bit of an aphrodisiac, in
a funny sort of way ... No ... I didn't want it that night because I didn't want
to be part of your scheme ... Oh, I know we were still making the rules, but
it wasn't fair to use me to ease your conscience.
Boy Ralph (*off*) Marcy?
Ralph Did we do it?
Marcia What do *you* think?
Boy Ralph (*off*) Come on.
Ralph Where?
Marcia Guess.

Girl Marcia walks off into the bathroom

The Lights change

Ralph Has that happened often?

Marcia What?

Ralph How many times have you done it when you didn't really want to?

Marcia How many times have you lied to me?

Ralph Not so many lately.

Marcia Maybe we come out about even then.

Ralph (*standing and moving* R *of the dressing-table*) And they've only been little white ones.

Marcia I don't believe in those. A lie is a lie whatever its shade.

Ralph All right, innocent ones.

Marcia (*going back to sit at the dressing-table*) No such thing.

Ralph That's not true. There's nothing wrong in a little lie if it makes for a bit of fun, or a nice surprise. Could even save a lot of pain.

Marcia You never used to think like that. Is that what forty years have done?

Ralph You can't expect to stay the same.

Marcia Why not?

Ralph Because you can't. (*Slight pause*) I've changed, you have too.

Marcia Yes, you're right ... We're not the same as we were. (*Slight pause*) I suppose we're *similar* ... but different in certain respects.

Ralph (*smiling*) Shouldn't we be getting on?

Marcia And that hasn't changed ... your smile. That's just the same. (*Slight pause before going to the wardrobe*) I never found out who she was.

Ralph (*topping up his own drink*) It wasn't anyone you knew. She was just someone who worked on the Boots counter.

Marcia (*taking out three dresses, one of them made from very shiny silver material*) A bank clerk's bit of rough, eh?

Ralph (*almost laughing*) If you like ... it never meant anything.

Marcia (*placing the dresses on the bed*) I often wondered why our bathroom cabinet was always full of corn plasters.

Ralph (*laughing*) I had to buy *something* every time I went in there, it could hardly be condoms.

Marcia Why not? She could probably get them cost.

Ralph (*laughing again*) You're a girl.

His laughter fades as he sees Marcia's stony face. She takes one of the dresses and holds it up to herself in the imaginary dressing-table mirror

Ralph (*moving* L) How do I know you haven't had an extra marital?

Marcia You don't.

Ralph Have you?

Marcia That's for me to know.

Ralph It's all right if you have.

Marcia Of course it is ... from the moment you did it, it was in the rules.

Ralph Tell me then.

Marcia No.

Ralph Would you if you had?

Marcia (*deciding against the dress, returning it to the bed*) Why do you want to know?

Ralph I told you about mine.

Marcia No you didn't, *I* told you about yours. (*She chooses another dress and returns to the mirror*)

Ralph (*sitting in the chair*) Tell me who, when, I want to know how long ago.

Marcia Last month. What do you think about this?

Ralph Last month?

Marcia Does that make you feel better? It's what you wanted to hear, wasn't it? (*Meaning the dress*) Is this right or not?

Ralph Last month?

Marcia At least it evens up the score from your point of view ... eases the conscience a bit. No, I don't want to over dress. (*She returns the dress to the bed*)

Ralph (*standing*) Last month?

Marcia What's the matter? Me seeing someone else is all right, it's the fact that it's so recent that bothers you?

Ralph It's just a blow that's all. I had no idea. What happened to us being honest with each other?

Marcia Shouldn't I be asking *you* that?

Ralph *Are* you seeing someone else?

Marcia Ralph, if I was having an affair I'd have to be seeing them.

Ralph But you haven't said you are having an affair!

Marcia No, I haven't, have I? And I haven't said I'm not either. (*She crosses and drinks the last of her champagne*) Do you know, if I drink any more of this I shan't be able to eat a thing. I'm glad it's Chinese, I could just about kill for a duck in plum sauce.

There is a slight pause as he looks at her. Then he decides she was winding him up

Ralph (*smiling*) You had me going there for a minute.

Marcia It's so easy, Ralph.

Ralph You enjoy it, don't you? Messing about?

Marcia I love it.

Ralph (*sitting in the chair*) And that affair thing? That was only messing about as well.

Marcia (*crossing to him*) Shall I tell you something that bothers me? Why was it all right for *you* to have had an affair albeit thirty odd years ago because that was the arrangement we had then, but it wouldn't be all right for *me* to have one now? Have the rules changed without me knowing?

Ralph I didn't say it wouldn't be all right if you had an affair.

Marcia So it would then?

Ralph Why now? Why didn't you have one when I did?

Marcia What — *because* you did?

Ralph You said you knew about it at the time.

Marcia Perhaps I didn't want one then. Perhaps I was biding my time.

Ralph For thirty-seven years?

Marcia All good things come to he who waits.

Ralph (*getting up*) So you *are* seeing someone?

Marcia I wouldn't have an affair out of revenge, Ralph.

Ralph What would your motive be?

Marcia What was yours?

Ralph (*after a slight pause*) I don't remember.

Marcia Oh, come on ... you can do better than that. (*Slight pause*) You can't answer me, can you? Do you want to know why? (*Slight pause*) You didn't have one. There *was* no reason ... no cause ... no "motive", as you put it. She was just there. She was easy. Where's the challenge ... the fight ... where's the excitement in that? She was nothing ... she meant nothing. She was no threat. That wouldn't do for me. (*Slight pause*) No, Ralph, I'm not having an affair. *If* I was having an affair it would be for all the reasons you didn't have. *When* I have an affair it'll be for all the right reasons, and believe me, it will be the biggest threat you've ever known.

Ralph You intend having one then?

Marcia (*looking in the dressing-table mirror*) I'm sixty-two, but I'm not bad for my age. Sure to God there's someone out there for me.

Ralph If there were, don't you think you would have found them by now.

Marcia (*going over to the bed*) Not really.

Ralph Why not?

Marcia Because I've never really looked.

Ralph Meaning you're looking now?

Marcia (*sitting on the bed*) Well not at this very minute, no, but I'm in the market for one, yes. Perhaps you could recommend someone.

Ralph Are you serious?

Marcia No, I'm being silly.

Ralph Of course you are.

Marcia (*trying not to laugh*) I'm sure you'd prefer it if it was someone you didn't know.

Ralph Why are you doing this? We're about to go out and celebrate forty years of marriage and you're talking about having an affair.

Marcia Ralph, after forty years, I can't think of a better time, can you?

Ralph We should have talked about this years ago.

Marcia Why, because it suited you better then?

Ralph Yes ... No! (*Becoming a little tongue-tied*) It's been forty years for God's sake.

Marcia As opposed to three when you had yours?

Ralph Things were different then.

Marcia I should say, I had the girls ... well at least I had one of them. If *I* had had an affair then, it would have had to have been the window cleaner.

Ralph It's not unheard of.

Marcia Ralph, please ... rough I'm not into, that's your department.

Ralph Gloria was not rough.

Marcia Aha. (*Moving towards the dressing-table*) You remember her name then.

Ralph Well, maybe it wasn't Gloria. I said the first name that came into my head.

Marcia Perhaps there were others. Maybe *Gloria* was the first of many?

Ralph Wouldn't you have known being the Miss Marple you undoubtedly are?

Marcia So I'm wrong, then? You haven't cheated all your life?

Ralph No.

Marcia Of course you have ... we both have.

Ralph What?

Marcia We've cheated each other, Ralph. Oh, we thought what we did back then was very clever ... but all we did was short change each other ... and it's like it says in all the supermarkets, "Check your change because mistakes cannot be rectified". What time is it? (*She checks her watch then crosses to the bed where she picks up the silver dress*)

Ralph (*after a pause*) Am I going to lose you?

Marcia (*again, holding it against her in front of the imaginary dressing-table mirror*) What do you think of this?

Ralph You'll look like a fish.

Marcia A mermaid you mean?

Ralph Actually, I was thinking more of a tuna.

Marcia Don't be unkind ... A sprat maybe. Yes ... It's only a restaurant we're going to but you never know ... I could catch myself a mackerel.

Ralph (*putting his glass down on the dressing-table*) I'd be careful if I were you ... you could also fall overboard.

Marcia Meaning?

Ralph Forget it .... (*He is about to leave the room*) Where we're going tonight, the only thing you're likely to catch is a glimpse of the past.

He leaves

Marcia (*calling after him*) What's that supposed to mean? Ralph? Ralph!

Suddenly Boy Ralph comes in through the door. The Lights change and there is a sound effect

Marcia looks at him briefly before crossing to the telephone, throwing the dress on the bed as she goes. Boy Ralph takes off his jacket and places it over the chair before sitting in it. Marcia dials

(*Into the phone*) Yes, can you give me the number for Stephano's, please. ... Stephano's. (*Spelling the name*) S. T. E. P. H. ... It's a Chinese restaurant. ... Are you sure? It is new. Nothing. Well, thanks for trying. (*She hangs up and wonders about it for a second*) Something's definitely up.

Ralph comes back into the room. He ignores Marcia as he takes a tie from the rack which is hanging on the front of his wardrobe. He immediately begins to tie it as he bends down to see his reflection in the imaginary dressing-table mirror

(*Going to him*) Oh, you're not wearing *that* tie, are you?

Ralph Why else would I be putting it on?

Marcia (*standing beside him; holding the tie up by its widest end*) I can think of at least one other reason. (*It now resembles a noose*)

Ralph I like it.

Marcia It's a bit glum.

Ralph I feel glum.

Marcia You've got far nicer ones.

Ralph This reflects the way I feel perfectly.

Marcia It doesn't match up.

Ralph Story of my life.

Marcia Let me choose another one for you.

Ralph This is fine.

Marcia (*at his wardrobe*) Here you are.

Ralph (*raising his voice*) I said it's fine!

Marcia (*after a slight pause*) Are you upset?

Ralph What do *you* think.

Marcia Is it me?

He doesn't answer

Is it something I've said?

Ralph You'd think after forty years you wouldn't rock the boat.

Marcia After forty years I'm amazed we haven't run aground.

Ralph Not with me at the helm.

Marcia God, Ralph, you don't know your bow from your stern.

Ralph I can't stand these nautical metaphors.
Marcia You started it.

He draws breath to say something, then thinks better of it

What?

He shakes his head

What have I said?
Ralph (*moving* DR) All right, maybe things haven't been wonderful lately.
Marcia Huh! (*She undoes her dressing-gown as she goes to her wardrobe*)
Ralph I suppose you'd prefer it if I said they've never been great.
Marcia (*taking out another dress*) At least you'd be speaking the truth.
Ralph Tell me what it's been then? It must have been something better than crap or otherwise we wouldn't be here now talking about it.
Marcia (*slipping off her dressing-gown and hanging it on the wardrobe door*) It's been OK.
Ralph OK?
Marcia Yes, OK! (*Putting on the dress*) It could have been worse ... but let's face it, it could have been a hell of a lot better.
Ralph I thought you were happy.
Marcia Dear God, what made you think that? I survive, Ralph. Very nicely if you only look on the surface and that's all you've ever done. (*Slipping on a pair of shoes*) But after forty years the veneer is wearing a little thin, in fact it's beginning to crack.
Ralph Maybe you should have an affair with a french polisher.
Marcia (*taking her dressing-gown and hanging it on the bathroom door*) Right now I think I'd settle for a *shoe* polisher.
Ralph Are you that desperate?
Marcia Gives you some idea.
Ralph What can someone else give you that I can't?
Marcia What, apart from stimulating company, companionship and wonderful sex?
Ralph You're looking for all those things?
Marcia Didn't *you*? I know it's thirty-odd years ago but I assumed *Gloria* provided all that.
Ralph I told you, she didn't mean anything. It was just a fling. It didn't even last that long.
Marcia Eighteen months.
Ralph What?
Marcia You first saw her in March, and it all wrapped up a year the following September. The sixteenth of September, right?

Ralph I don't remember the date.
Marcia I do ... and do you want to know why?

*Girl Marcia comes into the bedroom carrying two envelopes. There is a
sound effect. She sees Boy Ralph sitting in the chair and goes to him*

Girl Marcia Many happy returns.
Ralph (*sitting on the telephone side of the bed*) My birthday. (*He looks up
and forces a rather sad smile*)
Girl Marcia A card from me and one from Cathy. (*She hands them to him*)
Marcia (*sitting at the dressing-table*) You often used to come and sit up here
before you had your bath.
Girl Marcia She wanted to give it to you herself but you didn't come home
in time ... she tried to keep awake but sleep got the better in the end.

Boy Ralph opens Cathy's card

Ralph I've still got it you know ... the card. (*He looks for it, finds it and takes
it out of the bedside cabinet*)
Marcia I know.
Girl Marcia She made it herself in school. (*Slight pause*) Do you want to
eat before or after your bath?
Boy Ralph I've already eaten.
Marcia I'd cooked a birthday supper.
Ralph Had you?
Boy Ralph I had a meeting ... one thing led to another and when they realized
it was my birthday, well ... you know how it is.
Ralph How did you know it finished that particular night?
Girl Marcia Better have your bath then.

Boy Ralph walks off into the bathroom

Girl Marcia's actions match perfectly Marcia's memories

Marcia You went for your bath and I went and hung up your jacket. I don't
usually look through your clothes but it had something heavy in one of the
pockets.

Girl Marcia takes out a package and opens it

It was a large bottle of cologne ... in a Boots' bag. (*The significance of it
being a Boots' bag has only just hit home*) The next time I saw it, it was face
down in the pedal bin. I knew it was over when you threw that away and
kept the card.

Ralph If it's any consolation it was me who called it a day.

Marcia It isn't.

Ralph (*after a slight pause*) I had no idea about the meal. Why didn't you say something?

Marcia Not my style. (*Slight pause. She gets up*) I was going to leave that week. I had it all planned only you never opened my card ... if you had it would have read, "To Ralph, Happy Birthday. The jig is up. Marcia". (*She laughs ironically*) Then I remember I almost shouted it at you.

Girl Marcia (*shouting; moving* UC) Ralph?

Boy Ralph (*off*) Yes?

A pause

Ralph Why didn't you?

Girl Marcia (*after a slight pause*) Nothing.

Girl Marcia leaves the room with the jacket

The Lights change

Ralph What changed your mind?

Marcia I don't know. Even now I don't know, and I often think about it.

Ralph Was that the only time you've thought of leaving me?

Marcia God no. I used to think about it at least once a month in those days.

Ralph And now?

Marcia Once a week.

Ralph (*laughing*) There you go again. (*He looks up at her and stops laughing*) How come you never did leave?

Marcia (*moving to the chair*) There's still time.

Ralph Answer me.

Marcia Somehow there was always a reason not to. (*Slight pause*) Do you remember the time when I wouldn't come away with you to some seminar in Munich or Brussels or where ever it was?

Boy Ralph comes out of the bathroom, followed by Girl Marcia. Again, the Lights change and there is a sound effect

Boy Ralph It's only for a couple of days.

Girl Marcia I don't want to go.

Ralph I never understood why.

Boy Ralph It'll be great, and we could both do with a break.

Girl Marcia No.

Marcia I suppose I should have told you why then.

Boy Ralph Cathy won't be a problem, we can make arrangements for her.
Ralph Tell me now.
Marcia I was pregnant.
Girl Marcia (*sitting at the dressing-table*) Cathy is staying with friends this
   weekend anyway.
Boy Ralph So what's the big deal?
Girl Marcia I plan to go away for a few days myself.
Boy Ralph (*sitting next to her*) Where?
Marcia It didn't matter. I was going to have a termination.
Ralph Why?
Marcia I didn't want your baby.
Boy Ralph Who are you going away with?
Girl Marcia No-one.
Ralph Did you hate me that much?
Marcia I didn't hate you at all. I just didn't want your baby.
Girl Marcia Honestly ... no-one. Don't look like that. No pressure,
   remember?
Boy Ralph Yeah ... I remember.
Marcia We had this row.
Ralph I haven't forgotten.
Girl Marcia (*shouting*) Why are you shouting?
Boy Ralph Because I'm bloody angry, that's why.
Marcia I said something like ——
Girl Marcia *You* go away all the time.
Ralph You were forever throwing that up.
Boy Ralph I go away twice a year with my job.
Ralph Which was true.
Girl Marcia So you say.
Boy Ralph Ring the bloody bank if you want to.
Marcia As if.
Ralph It would have made it a lot easier if you had.
Boy Ralph Look, would I be asking you to come away with me if I was going
   for a dirty weekend with someone else?
Ralph A very good point.
Girl Marcia Yes.
Boy Ralph What?
Girl Marcia Of course you would, Ralph.
Marcia You knew I wouldn't go.
Ralph Not for sure.
Boy Ralph I'd be taking a hell of a chance.
Girl Marcia I reckon you'd risk it.
Ralph What if you'd said ——
Boy Ralph Yes, all right I'll come?

Marcia Easy ——
Girl Marcia You'd let the other girl down.
Marcia And then you'd said ——
Boy Ralph What about our deal?
Girl Marcia Our pact to be honest with each other?
Ralph And I said ——
Marcia No ... I said ——
Girl Marcia What about it?
Boy Ralph I wouldn't lie to you.
Marcia Do you remember that?
Girl Marcia Wouldn't you?
Ralph No.
Marcia That was four years after your affair with the shop girl.
Boy Ralph I wouldn't ... even though I'm sure you're not being honest with
    me.
Marcia I couldn't believe you said that.
Ralph I don't think I did.
Marcia You did. Believe me ... you had a nerve.
Ralph I think I said ——
Marcia And then you went on to say ——
Boy Ralph You're *not* being honest, are you?
Ralph And you weren't.
Girl Marcia (*insisting*) I am going away on my own.
Marcia (*also insisting*) Which I was.
Girl Marcia If I was taking anyone with me ——
Marcia Which I wasn't.
Girl Marcia —— I would tell you.
Marcia Believe me, Ralph, I would have loved to have said I'm sorry I can't
    go with you to Brussels because I am buggering off with someone nice for
    a couple of days.
Boy Ralph Is there anything I can say to make you change your mind?
Marcia I was booked into a clinic. Nothing would have moved me.
Girl Marcia No.

Boy Ralph storms out. Girl Marcia also leaves the room

The Lights change. Pause

Ralph (*standing*) So, I went to Brussels and you went to wherever it was.
Marcia You never did ask me where when you got back.
Ralph I figured if you wanted me to know you'd have said.
Marcia (*sitting at the dressing-table*) You were very cool as I remember.
Ralph As only you could ... So what happened then?

Marcia When?

Ralph When you went to wherever it was.

Marcia (*sitting in the armchair*) What do you mean, what happened?

Ralph (*moving to her*) Well something must have, we had two children the last time I counted.

Marcia Oh ... well, when push came to shove, I couldn't go through with it.

Ralph I don't suppose I could flatter myself by thinking I featured in any way in your decision?

Marcia I can't lie to you, Ralph.

Ralph You lied about that weekend.

Marcia No, I didn't. I just didn't tell you the whole truth, that's all.

Ralph Sounds suspiciously like a little white lie to me. Odd coming from someone who doesn't believe in them.

Marcia I'm not going to argue with you, Ralph.

Ralph Because you know you're wrong. When you think you're right you fight to the bitter end.

Marcia Yes, I do, don't I?

Ralph You still haven't answered me. What changed your mind?

Marcia It's a long time ago.

Ralph An important decision like that and you're telling me you can't remember your reason for making it?

Marcia I didn't say that, I just said it was a long time ago.

Ralph It's what you implied. Answer me.

Marcia Would you believe me if I told you I thought it wasn't yours?

Ralph (*after a slight pause*) Yes ... no ... I don't know. (*Slight pause*) Is she mine?

Marcia Oh, yes.

Ralph But you weren't sure at the time?

Marcia No.

Ralph So you did have an affair?

Marcia No, Ralph. I didn't have an affair. I didn't even have a fling. It was one of those one-night things. I'd tell you about it but I was so damned drunk at the time ——

Ralph You've forgotten all about it.

Marcia Well, not everything.

Ralph Would you remember who it was?

Marcia Oh, yes.

Ralph Would *I* remember who it was?

Marcia Of course.

Ralph It's someone we both knew then?

Marcia Well, I didn't know him very well at the time.

Ralph Well enough.

Marcia Apart from his name there is only one other thing I can remember about him.

Ralph I don't think I want to know that.

Marcia Well, that's all right then because I wasn't going to tell you anyway. At your time of life it wouldn't be fair to give you an inferiority complex. (*She laughs at her own joke*)

Ralph (*moving* DR) That's not funny.

Marcia Good, you're beginning to tell the difference.

Ralph (*after a slight pause*) I don't like you tonight.

Marcia Oh, I don't think I've liked me for a long time.

Ralph I think we'd better put all this behind us ... if only for now.

Marcia I've had enough of, "Putting it behind us", Ralph. Why can't we put it smack in front of us just for the hell of it?

Ralph Are you drunk?

Marcia You think I'd have to be, wouldn't you?

Ralph I don't want anything going wrong.

Marcia What do you mean, wrong?

Ralph Not tonight. Whatever happens, people mustn't suspect a thing.

Marcia What people?

Ralph As far as everyone is concerned, we're still the happy couple.

Marcia Who's everyone?

Ralph (*going to the dressing-table*) It's taken a lot of organizing. Judith and Cath have worked very hard. The last thing I want is to upset them.

Marcia I wish I knew what you were talking about.

Ralph They've been organizing it for weeks.

Marcia Organizing what for God's sake?

Ralph (*after a slight pause*) I wasn't being exactly truthful when I said we were going to Stephano's

Marcia I knew I had the name from you, Oh, don't tell me ... we're not eating Chinese either?

Ralph It wasn't my idea ... it was the girls who thought of it. They've organized a surprise.

Marcia I don't like surprises.

Ralph I know that and they do, but they thought this was different.

Marcia In what way?

Ralph Well, they thought this was different, that's all.

Marcia What have they organized?

Ralph Don't spoil it for them.

Marcia It's not a party, is it?

Ralph Well, sort of.

Marcia It is, isn't it?

Ralph They thought you'd be thrilled. Everybody's going to be there.

Marcia Please don't tell me they've gone and dug people up from God knows where.

Ralph Wouldn't you like to see Clive and Barbara?

Marcia (*with mock enthusiasm*) Clive and Barbara ... Malcolm and Eileen?

Ralph (*joining in enthusiastically*) Yes, Malcolm and Eileen. Wouldn't it be nice to see them all again?

Marcia I can't think of anything worse.

Ralph There'll be lots of other people there as well.

Marcia Sounds like my worst nightmare.

Ralph Come on ... it's not as bad as all that.

Marcia What the hell made them do it?

Ralph It was Cathy who suggested we shouldn't let the occasion pass.

Marcia I'll kill her.

Ralph It started out with it just being a few close friends ... no-one thought for a minute it was going to stretch to three to four hundred.

Marcia (*amazed*) What?

Ralph Don't worry ... not everyone will turn up.

Marcia I don't believe this. Why did you let them do it?

Ralph I said you wouldn't be keen but they talked me round. Don't you think it might be fun?

Marcia (*sitting on the stool*) How long have you known about this?

Ralph I'm not sure.

Marcia How long?

Ralph Well, from the start, really.

Marcia What were you thinking of?

Ralph I suppose I thought part of you would go along with it ... perhaps even enjoy it.

Marcia Living a lie is one thing ... acting it out in front of hundreds of people *for* hundreds of people is something completely different.

Ralph The girls weren't to know.

Marcia They had a bloody good idea.

Ralph (*after a slight pause*) What, you mean they know how you feel?

Marcia They know the score, yes.

Ralph You've discussed it with them?

Marcia Women do you know ... Mothers, daughters ... girl-talk, come on.

Ralph You mean they actually know how we really live?

Marcia They've known about it for years, Ralph. Which makes me think all the more that this is some kind of wind-up.

Ralph They wouldn't do that.

Marcia Why else would they do it?

Ralph Forty years is a long time ... it deserves to be marked.

Marcia It depends from which end you look at it.

Ralph (*after a pause*) Has it really been that bad?

Marcia You've no idea, have you?

Ralph I don't understand why you're still here then.

Marcia I'm not ... not really. I left years ago.

Ralph Then that's sad.

Marcia The tragedy isn't that I left, Ralph ... it's you never knew I'd gone.

Ralph (*after a slight pause*) Well, of course you can come back.

Marcia Ah, but do I want to? What's here for me to come back to?

Ralph What there's always been here.

Marcia Exactly. (*She stands and moves* R *of Ralph*) Look, this thing tonight is an absolute mockery and when I see the girls I shall tell them.

Ralph No, don't do that. If they knew the score like you said, all they did was humour me. It makes sense now why they didn't seem keen.

Marcia But you said ... They didn't have anything to do with it!

Ralph No ... blame anyone, blame me.

Marcia You did it?

Slight pause, he doesn't answer

Why?

Ralph Why do you think? (*Slight pause*) OK, I got it wrong, but it's too late now... unless you want to ring The Moat House Hotel and send everyone home.

Marcia I can't believe you'd do this to me.

Ralph I did it with the best intentions

Marcia (*shouting*) Fiascos usually are.

Ralph It's not going to be a fiasco.

Marcia (*even louder*) Ralph ... it already is.

They stare at each other for a moment. Ralph breaks it

Ralph I'm going downstairs.

Marcia For a drink?

Ralph It might help.

Marcia It's not the answer.

Ralph Do you want one?

Marcia (*screaming after him*) No!

He goes

Marcia is frustrated as hell. In her temper she quickly gathers the dresses from the bed and throws them to the foot of the wardrobe

Suddenly the Lights change and there is a sound effect as Girl Marcia comes out of the bathroom wearing pyjamas. She sits at the dressing-table

Marcia slowly walks over towards her. She stands immediately behind, looking down at her

Boy Ralph comes into the bedroom also wearing pyjamas. He carries two glasses of whisky. There is a sound effect

Marcia takes a step or two back

Boy Ralph hands Girl Marcia the drink. She pulls him towards her and kisses him before swallowing the drink down in one. He puts his drink on the dressing-table

God ... I could put it away even then.

Boy Ralph (*moving to the bike*) I rang you a couple of times today but you weren't here.

Girl Marcia You don't usually ring from work.

Boy Ralph I know .. but you were on my mind for some reason.

Marcia For a minute I thought he tumbled it.

Boy Ralph mounts the exercise bike and pedals gently for a moment or two

Boy Ralph The girls said you weren't even in the house when they came in from school.

Girl Marcia I got back about five.

Boy Ralph Where did you go, somewhere nice?

Marcia But then I knew he didn't have a clue.

Girl Marcia I had an appointment.

Boy Ralph You didn't say. (*He begins to pedal much faster now*)

Marcia (*insisting*) I did!

Girl Marcia I did, but it never registered.

Boy Ralph The girls were worried sick.

Girl Marcia And you?

Marcia I knew he wouldn't answer.

Boy Ralph What's my target on this, can you remember?

Girl Marcia No.

Boy Ralph I think I'm up to a mile ——

Girl Marcia I was at the hospital.

Boy Ralph At fifteen miles an hour. (*He tries to pedal faster*)

Marcia I wish to God I hadn't mentioned it now.

Girl Marcia A couple of weeks ago I found a lump.

She pauses but there is no reaction from Boy Ralph

Marcia He could have said *something*.

Girl Marcia They did tests and it's not good news.

Boy Ralph I reckon that's about five minutes at this speed if I can keep it up.

Girl Marcia (*putting a hand on one of her breasts*) I have to have it removed.

Again there's no reaction from him

(*Raising her voice slightly*) Did you hear me? I'm going to have surgery!

He's been concentrating on his pedalling and has now begun to break out in a sweat. He wipes his forehead with the back of his hand as he looks over at Girl Marcia and smiles

Boy Ralph Are you timing me?

Girl Marcia goes to the bed, takes a pillow and hits him so hard that he almost loses his balance on the bike

Marcia Did I really do that?
Boy Ralph (*breathless*) What was that for?
Girl Marcia I was trying to tell you something.
Boy Ralph Couldn't it have kept?
Girl Marcia You can go on that at any time.
Boy Ralph It doesn't work like that. You should get on this yourself ... you're starting to spread a bit.
Girl Marcia I don't *believe* you!
Marcia (*looking at herself in the dressing-table mirror*) I should have listened to him.
Boy Ralph What have I said? You'd want me to tell you, don't you?
Girl Marcia What?
Boy Ralph That you're putting on a bit of weight.
Girl Marcia You're incredible, you know that?
Boy Ralph It's our age. I'd be the same if I didn't watch it.
Marcia (*shouting*) Why the hell didn't I listen to him!
Boy Ralph So what is it?
Girl Marcia What?
Boy Ralph That you wanted to tell me.
Girl Marcia (*sitting on the bed*) It's not important.
Boy Ralph No, no ... it was important enough for you to almost knock me off my bike. What is it?
Girl Marcia I don't want to tell you now.
Boy Ralph (*getting off the bike*) Oh, well ... please yourself.
Marcia That's right, if at first you don't succeed — give up.
Girl Marcia You obviously don't want to know.
Boy Ralph (*picking up his drink from the dressing-table*) This is a silly conversation.

Girl Marcia You know, for someone who is supposed to be intelligent, you've got no idea of the difference between the silly and the serious!

Marcia And he still hasn't.

Boy Ralph What is it with you? I've asked you to tell me what it was, and then you accuse me of not wanting to know.

Girl Marcia I'd rather you left it there. I'll deal with it on my own.

Boy Ralph Fine.

Marcia (*shouting*) Press me for God's sake!

Boy Ralph If that's what you'd prefer.

Girl Marcia (*almost under her breath*) I'll find some other shoulder to lean on.

Boy Ralph What?

Girl Marcia Nothing. If I were you I'd get back on that thing. (*She indicates the bike*) Your waist is growing in front of me.

Boy Ralph You really are ——

Girl Marcia What?

Boy Ralph (*after a slight pause*) Nothing.

Girl Marcia What?

Boy Ralph (*after a slight pause*) What's happening to us?

Girl Marcia To *me* you mean.

Boy Ralph I didn't say you.

Girl Marcia Perhaps *I* mean me, then.

Marcia Yes.

Boy Ralph Is there something going on?

Marcia I should have told him then.

Boy Ralph Tell me.

Girl Marcia One day.

Boy Ralph It's not important?

Both Marcias look at him

Well, it can't be if you don't want to talk about it now.

Marcia But I did!

Girl Marcia You really do drive me up the wall sometimes.

Girl Marcia goes off into the bathroom

A slight pause

Boy Ralph (*calling to her*) Perhaps you should go and see someone.

Girl Marcia appears from the bathroom

Girl Marcia Me?

Marcia He meant a shrink.
Boy Ralph You're the one who seems to have a problem.
Marcia I do, but my problem is you.
Boy Ralph That's not fair, what have *I* done?

Girl Marcia goes back into the bathroom

Girl Marcia (*as she goes*) You never listen to what I say.
Boy Ralph (*following her*) That's not true.

Boy Ralph goes into the bathroom

The Lights change and there is a sound effect

Marcia squeezes her fists and makes a noise in frustration. As she crosses the room she catches sight of herself in the imaginary dressing-table mirror. She turns sideways and holds herself in. She then goes to the exercise bike and pedals frantically for a few seconds. She can't keep it up for long. She stops and folds her arms in frustration

Ralph comes back into the bedroom having been downstairs. He is carrying two glasses of whisky. He spots her still sitting on the bike

Ralph What are you doing on that?
Marcia It's called psychological exercising. I sit here and imagine I'm burning up calories.
Ralph Does it work?
Marcia I'm a size twelve ... in my head.

He offers her a drink

No.
Ralph I thought perhaps you'd change your mind. (*He offers the drink again*)
Marcia I said no.

A pause as he places her drink on the dressing-table

Ralph It hasn't been all bad.

She looks over at him

Us.

She pauses then looks away again

It hasn't.

Marcia What has it been then?

Ralph (*after a slight pause*) When I think of some of the others ——

Marcia Tell me what it's been.

Ralph Regardless of what you say it hasn't been purgatory.

Marcia (*getting off the bike*) Tell me what it's been not what it hasn't.

Ralph Well, under the circumstances ——

Marcia Exactly! Under the circumstances there shouldn't be any circumstances.

Ralph But there were. And it's all of our own making and there's nothing we can do about it.

Marcia (*quietly*) Tell me what it's been.

Ralph It's been forty years, that's what it's been. (*Slight pause*) It's *been* good.

Marcia Then why am I so thoroughly miserable?

Ralph Because you don't know what you want.

Marcia I do know what I want. I know *exactly* what I want ... and I haven't had it.

Ralph (*after a slight pause*) Do you think you're heading for some sort of breakdown?

Marcia (*laughing loudly in frustration*) He doesn't even ask what it is.

Ralph I'm sure it might be something like that, don't you?

Marcia And do you know why? Do you know why you're not asking me? It's because deep down we want the same thing. We do. The only difference between us is that you've buried your need. It's so far down you can't touch it any more ... sometimes you even managed to forget it's there ... but it's not like that for me. Mine is only just below the surface. Mine pops up from time to time ... mine won't *let* me forget! (*She pulls herself together*) Do you know what I think? I think you're dead ... but that's not so bad. In a funny sort of way that makes you the lucky one.

Ralph Dear God, what have I done to you?

Marcia You haven't done anything to me that I haven't let you do ... and that makes it worse. I can't do what you've done, Ralph.

Ralph What's that.

Marcia Close down. Shut up shop.

Ralph's reaction is one of disagreement

Yes, that is what you've done.

Ralph I don't understand you any more.

Marcia You're never understood me, that's always been the problem. Open your eyes, Ralph. Reach down ... get in touch with yourself.

Ralph No.

Marcia Afraid?

Ralph In a way ... if I did that I'd be like you.

Marcia Alive.

Ralph And miserable ... and lonely. If I felt like you we wouldn't be together.

Marcia Dear God, you think we're together now?

Ralph After a fashion.

Marcia And that's good enough for you?

Ralph It's better than the alternative.

Marcia Don't you know what you've missed?

He doesn't answer

Of course you don't.

Ralph We've been together for the most part of our lives.

Marcia We've shared this house for most of our lives.

Ralph Doesn't that stand for anything?

Marcia When I think of it, it makes me cry.

Ralph (*sincerely*) Well, thanks for that, anyway.

Marcia (*almost getting upset*) I didn't mean it like ... Oh ... God ...

Ralph I love you.

Marcia (*shouting*) No!

Ralph What do you mean, "no"?

Marcia (*sitting at the dressing-table*) You can't.

Ralph I'm sorry if it's not what you want to hear, but it's how I feel.

Marcia We're not supposed to say it. We never say it.

Ralph Well, I just did.

Marcia Tell me you didn't mean it.

Ralph Why? So that it'll make you feel better? No. I won't take it back, Marcy.

Marcia You'll never hear it from me.

Ralph I don't care ... I don't need to. (*Slight pause*) I love you.

Marcia No!

Ralph And when we walk into that hotel tonight, *if* we walk into that hotel tonight, people will look at us and think, "There's the happy couple", and that's OK. So what if they're only fifty per cent right.

Marcia You're not happy, Ralph. If you love me like you say you do, you can't be knowing how I feel.

Ralph There's more than one kind of love you know ... it's like those lies we talked about, it comes in a thousand different shades.

Marcia (*after a slight pause*) No, I can't go through with it. There's no way I could walk into that place tonight on your arm.

Ralph Would you prefer it if we arrived separately? I'm sure I could arrange it.

Marcia It's not funny.

Ralph (*after a slight pause*) You're right ... it's pathetic. (*Slight pause. He finishes off the second whisky*) Well, if you're not going you'd better ring and say. (*Checking his watch*) We're already late. I'm surprised someone hasn't picked up the phone to ask where we are. If they do, *you* can answer that one.

Marcia I don't expect you to understand.

Ralph That's all right then.

Marcia (*shouting*) Will you stop being so bloody reasonable!

Ralph You want me to rant and rave, is that it?

Marcia God no, you'd have to be alive for that.

Ralph Do you know what I don't understand about you? How it is you can make me laugh if you feel so sad?

Marcia How is it you never understood I wasn't being funny?

A slight pause. Suddenly the telephone rings. They both look at it before looking back at each other

Ralph For you, I think.

He leaves the room through the landing door

Marcia stands looking across the room at the telephone as it continues to ring

The rings get louder and louder as the Lights fade to a ——

BLACK-OUT

ACT II

The same. 8 p.m.

Everything is as it was at the end of Act I. Marcia is still in the same position

As the Lights come up, the telephone is still ringing loudly. After it has rung three or four times, it rings at the normal volume. Marcia turns away upstage having decided not to answer it

Suddenly the Lights change and there is a sound effect as Girl Marcia comes into the room from the landing. She crosses to the telephone and answers it

Girl Marcia (*into the phone*) Hallo? ... Who? ... I think he's still in the garden, can I ask him to ring you back?

Marcia comes to sit at the dressing-table

Congratulations?

Boy Ralph comes in from the landing wearing garden clothes. There is a sound effect. He crosses and goes straight out into the bathroom

Oh ... right. ... Yes. Yes. I'll tell him. (*She hangs up*) That was for you. Some Jimmy Taylor?

Boy Ralph puts his head round the bathroom door

Boy Ralph Shall I ring him back?
Girl Marcia He said it wasn't important ... he just wanted to congratulate you, that's all.

Boy Ralph comes into the room and moves towards the wardrobe

Boy Ralph I see.
Girl Marcia On your new job.
Boy Ralph Right.

Girl Marcia In London.
Boy Ralph Ah ...
Girl Marcia I suppose you were going to tell me.
Boy Ralph Would you believe it, tonight?
Marcia Bloody liar.
Boy Ralph Are you annoyed?
Girl Marcia Not at all.
Boy Ralph It's an excellent promotion.
Girl Marcia Congratulations.
Boy Ralph You're very good about it.
Girl Marcia Didn't you think I'd be pleased for you?
Boy Ralph I wasn't sure what your reaction would be.
Marcia I bet you weren't.
Girl Marcia Which is why you were dragging your feet about telling me.
Boy Ralph I wasn't dragging my feet. I was going to tell you over dinner.
Marcia I don't know why ... softeners like that never worked on me.
Boy Ralph You like London, don't you?
Girl Marcia Love it.
Boy Ralph Good. We'll sell this place and buy something really special.
Marcia (*smiling, closing her eyes*) I love this bit.
Girl Marcia No, you can't sell the house.
Boy Ralph Too many memories?
Marcia (*opening her eyes*) Now that's got to be the funniest thing he's ever said.
Boy Ralph All right, we'll rent it then.
Girl Marcia You can't do that either.
Boy Ralph Why not?
Marcia Here it comes.
Girl Marcia Because I'll be living in it.
Boy Ralph What?
Marcia The penny still didn't drop.
Boy Ralph (*after a slight pause*) No ... No I can't commute. The new job means we're going to have to live there.
Marcia As if I didn't know.
Girl Marcia And you were going to tell me about it tonight ... that was sweet.
Boy Ralph You *are* annoyed?
Marcia I wasn't annoyed, Ralph.
Girl Marcia (*shouting*) I'm bloody furious!
Boy Ralph All right, calm down.
Girl Marcia (*shouting*) You can't make that kind of decision on your own.
Boy Ralph So let's talk about it.
Girl Marcia Have you accepted the job?
Boy Ralph We can negotiate around this?

Girl Marcia (*raising her voice*) Have you accepted the job?
Boy Ralph Yes.
Girl Marcia Well then, what's to bloody talk about?
Boy Ralph Give yourself time ... you'll come round to the idea.
Girl Marcia Ralph ... I don't *want* to live in London, and I'm not *going* to live in London. (*Slight pause*) You didn't honestly think you could pull this off?
Boy Ralph I *thought* you might follow me anywhere.

Marcia and Girl Marcia laugh loudly, almost maniacally

Girl Marcia (*shouting*) Why? What the hell would make you think something like that?
Boy Ralph (*going to stand behind Girl Marcia*) You're upset. Look, if you don't want me to take the job, I won't.
Girl Marcia Of course I want you to take the job.
Boy Ralph You do?
Marcia Yes!
Girl Marcia More than you know.
Boy Ralph But you won't come to London?
Marcia Hooray!
Girl Marcia Got it in one.
Boy Ralph If I take it and you won't come to London we'll be living apart.
Marcia (*standing, moving towards Boy Ralph*) He's sharp ... I'll say that for him.
Boy Ralph What does that mean?
Girl Marcia You're an intelligent man, Ralph. Work it out for yourself.
Boy Ralph (*after a slight pause*) I'll turn it down then ... if it's what you want, I'll turn it down.
Girl Marcia You *know* what I want.
Boy Ralph (*sitting on the bed, stretching his hand out to touch hers*) Yes, but you're upset ... you didn't mean that.

Girl Marcia gets up and screams in frustration as she stomps out into the bathroom

Marcia (*to Boy Ralph*) I deserve a medal the size of a frying pan.

He gets up and leaves the room

The Lights change

Ralph comes in from the landing

Ralph Something's bothering me.

Marcia Join the club.

Ralph Earlier on ... when you told me about the termination ——

Marcia I can't talk about that now, Ralph.

Ralph I've got to know, it's important.

Marcia It happened twenty-five years ago. Why are you bothering about it now?

Ralph Because you only told me in the last twenty minutes.

Marcia All right, come on ... let's get it over with. What do you want to know?

Ralph (*after a slight pause*) You said you didn't go through with it because you thought Judith wasn't mine.

Marcia Because I thought she was someone else's, yes.

Ralph Which implies you *would* have gone through with it if you thought she was mine.

Marcia That sounds awful, doesn't it?

Ralph Am I right?

She doesn't answer

I want to know what happened.

Marcia I was going to tell you, Ralph. It was only fair.

Ralph So why didn't you?

Marcia I bumped into him again ... quite by chance. I'd just been to the clinic, I was about seven months' pregnant at the time. We had a cup of coffee together.

Ralph Before or after a trip round Mothercare?

Marcia If you're going to be facetious ...

Ralph Go on.

Marcia One thing led to another ——

Ralph As they do ——

Marcia And I told him I thought the baby was his.

Ralph Just like that?

Marcia There was a lot of hedging on my part.

Ralph Let me guess what happened next. He denied it, obviously ——

Marcia He didn't have to. He told me he'd only just come back from a clinic himself. His sperm count was practically nil and they were trying to do something for him and his wife.

Ralph Poor Marcia ... after all that you were stuck with a child of mine.

Marcia I never held it against Judith.

Ralph Well, isn't that big of you.

Marcia I didn't mean it like that, I meant ——

Ralph You meant you loved her in spite of me, I know what you meant.

Marcia I don't care what you think.

Ralph You never have.
Marcia Well, there you are. Can't you see how bitter and twisted we are?
Ralph *You* are.
Marcia All right, *I* am. I'm bitter and twisted ... I'm tired and I can't keep it up any more.
Ralph (*after a slight pause*) Tell me who he is.
Marcia What good would that do?
Ralph Is he dead?
Marcia No.
Ralph Still married?
Marcia Yes.
Ralph Children?

She doesn't answer

(*Asking again, louder this time*) Children?
Marcia (*shouting*) No ...
Ralph Tell me who he is.
Marcia No.
Ralph Is it him that's been between us all these years?
Marcia Don't be silly.
Ralph Well, someone has.
Marcia You still don't know, do you?

He looks at her

You have no idea. It's me, Ralph. You don't have to look any further than me ... (*Sitting down at the dressing-table*) And if you think about it, it always has been.

Girl Marcia comes in. The Lights change and there is a sound effect. She is dressed in a "mother of the bride" costume, complete with hat. The period is around 1973. She sits at the dressing-table

Ralph I've always tried to make you happy.
Marcia No, not always.
Ralph Well, for the most part.
Marcia (*sitting on the stool*) You've never understood me, Ralph.
Ralph If I had I think I might have given you up.

Slight pause. He sits in the chair as Marcia stares into the imaginary dressing-table mirror

(*Eventually*) What are you thinking about now?

Marcia About me ... Cathy.
Ralph What about the two of you?
Marcia She was so lucky ... or maybe luck had nothing to do with it. Maybe
  she wouldn't settle for anything less than chemistry.
Ralph Chemistry?
Marcia They loved each other so much ... they could barely keep their hands
  off one another.
Ralph I can think of a better word for it than that.

*Boy Ralph anxiously enters the room. There is a sound effect. He too is
almost dressed for the wedding. He carries on his shoes, tail-coat, cravat
and corsage for Girl Marcia*

Boy Ralph You ready? The first car is on its way. Cath's a bit nervous ... she
  wants a word before you leave.

Girl Marcia doesn't react

  Is there something wrong?
Marcia No ...
Ralph (*getting up from the chair*) Hey ... come on.
Boy Ralph You shouldn't be sitting in here all on your own anyway.
Girl Marcia I just wanted a minute to myself, that's all.
Ralph You're not worried about Cath, are you?
Girl Marcia No.
Boy Ralph What is it then?
Marcia It's nothing.
Boy Ralph (*sitting on the bed and putting on his shoes*) Don't shut me out.
Girl Marcia I'll be all right in a minute.
Ralph Tell me what's wrong.
Girl Marcia (*after a slight pause*) They're going to be happy, aren't they?
Boy Ralph Cathy and Paul? Of course they are. Paul's a nice lad. We like
  him, don't we?
Marcia (*to Ralph*) We seem to have run out of paper tissues. Will you get
  some for me from downstairs.

Ralph leaves

Boy Ralph Is that what this is all about?

She doesn't answer

  They're going to be fine ... why shouldn't they be? You're worrying about
  nothing.

Girl Marcia I'm not worried.
Boy Ralph OK, what are you then?
Marcia Tell him.
Girl Marcia She loves him to bits.
Boy Ralph Of course she does.
Girl Marcia They look right together.
Marcia Which they did for a while.
Boy Ralph Of course they do, everybody says so.
Girl Marcia I'm not concerned.
Boy Ralph So what are you?
Marcia Go on, tell him.
Girl Marcia They're going to have a long and happy life together.
Boy Ralph *I* think so.
Marcia Tell him.
Girl Marcia I can't imagine anything ever going wrong.
Boy Ralph So what are you fretting about?
Girl Marcia I'm not fretting.
Boy Ralph (*insisting*) Tell me what you are then?
Marcia (*blurting it out*) Jealous.
Girl Marcia (*after a slight pause*) Tired.
Marcia Coward. I was jealous. She had something I didn't. I wanted to feel the way she did and I was as green as hell.
Girl Marcia Yes. I'm just tired, that's all.
Marcia And the silly bugger accepted that. If only he'd pushed that little bit harder.

Ralph comes into the bedroom with a box of paper hankies

Boy Ralph Never mind ... you can have a nice long lay-in tomorrow.
Marcia (*getting up from the dressing-table*) Oh God, as if that would put everything right.

Ralph catches Marcia's last few words. Boy Ralph is dressing at the bed

Ralph Sorry?
Marcia Nothing. (*Taking the box*) Thanks.

Ralph takes off his tie and changes it for another. Marcia wipes her nose on a paper tissue. Boy Ralph knots his cravat in the dressing-table mirror, and Girl Marcia stands just behind checking her overall appearance

A pause

Ralph I forgot to ask: who was on the phone earlier?

Girl Marcia Has the hairdresser gone?
Marcia I don't know.
Boy Ralph I think so.
Ralph Didn't you answer it?
Girl Marcia All the flowers arrived?
Marcia No.
Boy Ralph Yes. Everything's gone like clockwork.

Boy Ralph almost kisses Girl Marcia but she moves away. Ralph doesn't pause at all

Ralph Why?

Girl Marcia arranges her hat or corsage

Marcia I didn't know what to say.
Ralph Why?
Marcia What *could* I say?
Ralph The truth.
Marcia No, I couldn't do that, and if you ask why again I shall scream.
Ralph (*after a slight pause*) Why?
Marcia Are you winding me up?
Ralph You didn't scream.
Marcia Oh, please, I'm not in the mood. (*She sits down at the dressing-table*)
Ralph So what's new.
Boy Ralph You should see Cath ... she looks beautiful.
Girl Marcia (*almost snarling*) And happy.
Boy Ralph That didn't sound right. Tell me what's wrong.
Ralph You've been heavy-going lately.
Marcia Lately?
Boy Ralph The last couple of weeks.
Ralph Well, months.
Boy Ralph All right, years.
Marcia At least you've noticed.
Boy Ralph You can't ignore something like that.
Marcia You've had a damned good try.
Ralph Look, I'm not sure what it is you're going through ——
Boy Ralph But I know things haven't been easy for you for a while.
Marcia Try aeons.
Girl Marcia If that wasn't true it *might* have been funny.
Ralph You can still make me laugh ... well, smile.
Girl Marcia Show *me* how to do it?
Marcia It's been so long I've forgotten.

Girl Marcia You've never made me laugh.
Ralph I did once.
Marcia When? It's been so long even *you've* forgotten.

Suddenly Boy Ralph and Girl Marcia break away. He puts his coat on

Ralph (*joining Marcia at the dressing-table*) I've got an idea. Why don't we
   sod the lot of them and bugger off somewhere tonight. Just the two of us.
Girl Marcia Ralph?
Marcia Why would I want to do that?
Ralph To get away ...
Girl Marcia Where do you see yourself ten years from now?

Marcia looks at him

Ralph Oh yes ... sorry. I forgot, it's *me* you want to get away *from*.
Boy Ralph I don't know ... still here I hope.
Ralph Well, why don't *you* bugger off then?
Marcia Don't be silly.
Girl Marcia Yes ... I thought you did. (*She makes to leave*)
Ralph What if *I* went?
Marcia Running away isn't going to make it better.
Ralph So let's face it.
Boy Ralph Where are you going?
Marcia OK.
Girl Marcia To see Cath.

   Girl Marcia leaves and Boy Ralph follows her

The Lights change

Ralph Together.
Marcia Right.
Ralph Not now though, tomorrow. Let's get tonight over with first.
Marcia You don't give up.
Ralph Will you change your mind?
Marcia I think I'll lock myself in the attic.
Ralph What for?
Marcia Well, for one thing I wouldn't have to answer the damned telephone.
Ralph Now who's running away.
Marcia And for another at least you can tell them the truth. "I'm sorry Marcia
   can't make it, she's looped the loop in the loft." (*She gets up and goes
   towards the bed*)

Ralph And that will placate everyone, will it?

Marcia I don't care what it'll do.

Ralph Not even to the girls?

Marcia (*laying down on the bed*) I can't worry about them now ... not feeling as I do.

Ralph Can't you imagine what it'll be like for them? I mean, they're there, now this minute ... mixing with all those people. How will they cope with you not turning up?

Marcia Judith and Cath will be fine ... they've got their husbands to hold their hands.

Ralph (*after a slight pause*) Cathy hasn't ... well, not for much longer. She and Paul are splitting up

Marcia (*after a slight pause; sitting up on the bed*) I'm surprised she's told you.

Ralph She didn't. Paul did.

Marcia Paul? That's odd, isn't it? Don't you think that's odd? He decides to leave his wife and he tells his father-in-law. God, he's even more complicated than I thought.

Ralph It's hard to imagine them not together. Especially when you think of how they were the day they got married. We both thought it was a match made in heaven.

Marcia Just goes to show ...

Ralph It proves one thing I suppose ... it doesn't matter what you have to start out ... it's what you end up with that *really* counts.

Marcia How can you say that after all we've said to each other.

Ralph (*moving* U *of the bed*) Well, it's true. Think about it. We're a damned sight better off now than what we were when we started out. And I'm not talking financial investments here.

Marcia I wish you wouldn't keep using the word "we" when you talk about my assets — and by assets *I* don't mean Income Bonds either. If you want to take stock that's fine ... but there's absolutely nothing in *my* bank book.

Ralph And there's me thinking we had a joint account.

She almost smiles and he spots it

Was that a smile? My God, there's life there yet.

Marcia Don't get excited, it was probably wind. (*She throws herself back down on the bed. A slight pause*) It's so easy for you, isn't it?

Ralph You think so? I love you and you don't love me back. What could be harder than that?

Marcia You don't love me, Ralph. You just ... Oh, I don't know ... you depend on me. You're used to having me around. We both know that's not the same thing.

Ralph You can't tell me how I feel. You can't even tell me how *you* feel.

Marcia I'm trying to.

Ralph You're so mixed up you don't *know* how you feel.

Marcia (*after a slight pause, sitting up again*) I suppose there's another woman.

Ralph Sorry?

Marcia Paul and Cathy.

Ralph No. Why are we talking about them?

Marcia How do you know?

Ralph He told me.

Marcia And you believe him?

Ralph Yes. We were talking about *us*.

Marcia Then that's a shame.

Ralph Why?

Marcia If you're walking away from a marriage then the best reason in the world should be because you've got someone nice tucked away somewhere.

Ralph And you'd wish that on Cathy?

Marcia If he's going off for a better life then maybe she will too.

Ralph This is all to do with you and me, isn't it?

Marcia I don't know ... is it?

Ralph If you're not happy, throwing in the towel isn't always the answer.

Marcia You're right, this is about us.

Ralph Well, it's not.

Marcia What's the point of hanging on in there if it's over.

Ralph It's not over till it's over.

Marcia What the hell is that supposed to mean?

Ralph Oh, I don't know.

Marcia Well, if I were Paul I wouldn't hang about. I'd get out as soon as I could.

Ralph You think you're qualified to give that kind of advice?

Marcia I think I'm the most qualified person I know.

Ralph You're very hard, you know.

Marcia No, I'm not, I'm honest and the truth is never easy. (*Slight pause*) If it's not another woman with Paul, what do you suppose the reason is for the split?

Ralph I don't want to say.

Marcia (*standing and moving to Ralph*) He asked you not to?

Ralph No.

Marcia Tell me then.

Ralph You don't want to know.

Marcia Would I be asking if I didn't?

Ralph I'd drop it if I were you.

Marcia No, I'm intrigued. Tell me why they're splitting.

Ralph All right. (*He pauses*) He said she's become too much like you.

Marcia Bastard. Now this might come as a surprise to you, but do you know what Cathy told me? Paul's not leaving her at all ... she's leaving him, and do you know why? Her words: "I can't stand it any more, he's getting so much like Daddy".

Ralph Obviously they're not communicating very well.

Marcia That *does* make them like us then.

Ralph I still say we're not as bad as you make out.

Marcia Ralph? (*Slight pause*) Will you do something for me?

Ralph Anything.

Marcia Well, it's not for me really, it's for you ... let me go.

Ralph (*after a slight pause*) You've always been free to go, you know that ... but I won't give you up without a fight.

Marcia Very gallant, but I don't want you to fight for me.

Ralph I wouldn't be ... I'd be fighting for myself.

Marcia Don't you think that would be too little too late?

Ralph It's never too late.

Marcia Give it up, Ralph. It doesn't work for us these days.

Ralph You admit it worked once then?

Marcia What?

Ralph You said, "It doesn't work for us these days". That implies you thought it did at one time.

Marcia We had a plan, we didn't stick to it ... and to be honest I don't think it would have worked even if we had ... in fact, I *know* it wouldn't have.

Ralph So ... what has living with me been like for you then?

Marcia (*raising her voice*) Don't pretend you don't know ... you know perfectly well what it's been like for me.

Ralph I want to hear you say it.

Marcia (*shouting*) A drudge! (*Quieter now*) It's been a drudge.

Ralph How can you say that after everything you've had?

Marcia Drudgery is drudgery however you wrap it up and there's only two ways of dealing with it ... you either get up and walk away or pretend it doesn't exist, like you, and I can't do that. We've never been there for each other. It's late in the day I know but I just can't go with the flow any more. (*She goes to the wardrobe and takes out a suitcase. She puts it on the bed and moves back and forth from bed to wardrobe and packs*)

Ralph What are you doing?

Marcia What does it look like.

Ralph You can't leave.

Marcia I can do whatever I want. We both can, it's the rules, remember?

Ralph Where will you go?

Marcia I don't know.

Ralph Look, can't we talk about this?

Marcia There's no point.
Ralph Please!
Marcia OK ... OK, you talk and I'll pack.
Ralph I don't deserve this.
Marcia We both don't.
Ralph (*moving* U) If you leave, I don't know what I'll do.

Marcia stops briefly. Pause

Marcia I hope that doesn't mean what I think it means.
Ralph I can't imagine my life without you.
Marcia (*screaming*) You're suffocating me, don't you see that?
Ralph Then let's talk to someone.
Marcia It wouldn't do any good.
Ralph *I* think it might.
Marcia But I don't.
Ralph Please don't do this.
Marcia Look at me.
Ralph I am looking at you.
Marcia No, I mean really look at me. (*Slight pause*) What do you see?
Ralph (*after a slight pause*) We can get through this.
Marcia (*shouting*) Tell me what you see!
Ralph (*shouting back*) I see a silly old woman! (*A pause. Quieter now*) I see a silly old woman who can't let go of something and who ought to know better.
Marcia (*after a slight pause*) Shall I tell you what I see?

He doesn't answer

When I look in the mirror I don't see anything. (*She comes to sit down at the dressing-table*) I don't know where I'm going, I only know where I've come from and what I've left behind. Do you have any idea how frightening that is?

He doesn't answer

I've missed out on so much ... all the things no-one should miss out on. (*Slight pause*) I don't know what it's like to kiss someone and feel my body fit to explode. I've no idea what it's like to look into someone's eyes and feel a thrill in my stomach when it turns over as if it was on a Big Dipper. No-one has ever taken my breath away ... I don't know what it's like to be hurt because in order to be hurt you have to be vulnerable ... and that's something I've never been.

Ralph (*after a slight pause*) I think you're the most vulnerable woman I know.

Marcia You must have missed those things too.

Ralph It's like you said ... I put them all away. (*Moving to Marcia*) OK, so we haven't had all the thrills and spills ... there've been compensations.

Marcia (*shouting*) You're doing it again. (*Getting up to take more clothes out the wardrobe*) You're talking about everything from your point of view.

Ralph It's what I'm used to, you never really express yours.

Marcia Of course I express myself ... it's just that most of the time you've either switched off or you think I'm making some kind of a joke.

Ralph Only because you say the most funny things when you're serious.

Marcia My way of dealing with it. I've been telling you for years how I feel about our marriage but you haven't been taking notice.

Ralph *My* way of dealing with it.

Marcia So you're aware of how I feel? This hasn't come as a total surprise then?

Ralph Well, yes, it has. I was aware we were having our ups and downs, but I had no idea how strongly you felt.

Marcia But you know now.

Ralph Oh yes ... on this occasion you've expressed yourself with perfect clarity.

Marcia Helped by the fact no doubt that for the first time you've actually listened to me.

Ralph Aren't we getting on well?

Marcia (*moving away in frustration*) What was it you said earlier about being sarcastic?

Suddenly the phone rings. They both hesitate. Marcia looks at Ralph before crossing to take underwear out of the dressing-table drawer. Ralph eventually answers the phone

Ralph (*into the phone*) Hallo? ... Oh, Cathy. I'm not sure. ... Really? (*Looking at his watch*) Is it that time already? Well, we've had a bit of a hitch.

Marcia (*resuming her packing*) Now that's an understatement.

Ralph No, that was your mother. Well, I suppose it's more of a crisis really. Difficult to say. (*He holds the receiver towards Marcia*) She wants a word.

Marcia shakes her head and waves her hands about

I'm sorry your mother can't come to the phone now, she's packing. ... No, it's nothing serious. ... Yes, of course, we'll be there.

Marcia takes the suitcase from the bed and struggles with it across the room

I don't know ... tell them we're on our way ... tell them anything. What? ... No, I don't want to talk to Malcolm or Eileen.

Marcia (*putting the case down*) Dear God!

Ralph No, don't put him on the phone. No, Cathy, no, I don't want to. ... Hallo, Malcolm, how are you? ... Good. ... Oh fine, yes. Look, we're running a bit late so I won't chat. ... Good, I'm glad they're looking after you. ... Yes of course Marcia knows you're there. ... Oh ... thrilled. ... Yes, I'll do that ... yes, and give my love to Eileen too. (*He replaces the receiver*)

Marcia Thrilled?

Ralph What else could I say?

She doesn't answer him

They seem to be having a good time already. He said the girls are looking after him. He'll enjoy that not having any kids of his ... Oh, shit! (*He sits on the bed*) It's him, isn't it? It's Malcolm. He's the one you ——

Marcia Did it with once, yes ... so now you know.

A pause

Ralph I don't know what to say.

Marcia You're not trying hard enough. Come on, I'm sure you can think of something.

Ralph (*after a slight pause*) Was he better than me?

Marcia Ralph, even I'm better than you on my own.

Ralph That's a bit cruel, isn't it?

Marcia Let's be honest, our sex-life is about as busy as Macey's Mini Market.

Ralph That's not there any more.

She just looks at him

You've never complained.

Marcia I'm not complaining *now*. Look, I'll collect the rest of my things some other time.

Ralph (*standing*) Why Malcolm?

Marcia I don't know. He was there and you weren't. Any port in a storm, I suppose.

Ralph (*after a slight pause*) I think I'm going to kill him.

Marcia Don't be silly. Anyway it wasn't his fault. I drank a bottle of Blue Nun, the poor bugger didn't know if he was coming or going ...

Ralph Where was I?

Marcia God knows. You weren't collecting corn plasters, I know that. That affair was well over by then. Will you carry this downstairs for me?

Ralph (*crossing to her*) Please don't do this? Not tonight. If you're going to leave, leave in the morning ... leave straight after the celebrations. You can't not turn up ... think about how many people you'll be letting down.

Marcia I can't think about anyone else any more, Ralph.

Ralph Have I ever asked you for anything?

Marcia Is this a trick question?

Ralph Have I?

Marcia Not really ... so you're going to ask me for something *now*, right?

Ralph If you won't do it for me, do it for the girls ... don't do it for yourself for God's sake. What will people think of you if I turn up on my own?

Marcia Don't you understand, I don't care?

Ralph (*shouting*) What the hell's happening to you?

Marcia (*shouting back*) I'm getting myself a life.

Ralph We've been together all this time, can't you get one tomorrow?

She laughs

It's not funny.

Marcia I'm sorry, Ralph, but if I didn't laugh I'd scream.

Ralph Won't you even think about what I've said? What's one more night?

Marcia Ah, but it's not just one ordinary old night, is it? You're not asking me to stay in with my feet up and watch the television.

Ralph I'm asking you to hang on in there for another couple of hours.

Marcia You're asking me to rub my face in it.

Ralph And mine too.

Marcia Exactly. Now, are you going to take my case downstairs, or am I?

She waits for him to move but he doesn't

Right. (*She attempts to do it herself*)

Ralph No, I'll do it.

Ralph takes the suitcase and leaves the room

After he has gone, Marcia sighs and turns back into the room in frustration

Suddenly the Lights change and there is a sound effect. The same music as at the opening of the play is heard from the stereo

Girl Marcia comes out of the bathroom wearing a dressing-gown. She is also wearing a towel wrapped around her head and a small towel round her neck. She looks identical to Marcia at the beginning of the play. Girl Marcia takes the small towel from around her neck and places it in the ali-baba basket. She then comes to sit down at the dressing-table

Marcia watches her

Boy Ralph is heard calling, off

Boy Ralph (*off*) Marcia? Marcy, where are you? Marcy?
Girl Marcia Yes? (*She gets up and turns off the stereo then returns to the dressing-table*)

After a moment Boy Ralph comes in carrying a bottle of champagne and two glasses. There is a sound effect. He too is dressed identically to Ralph at the beginning of the play

Boy Ralph (*on seeing Girl Marcia*) There you are ... why didn't you answer?
Girl Marcia I did. Champagne?
Boy Ralph (*setting the glasses down on the low table at the foot of the bed*) Yes, champagne ... why not. It's a bit of a milestone after all.
Girl Marcia Millstone.
Boy Ralph (*laughing*) Why do you say things like that, you know you don't mean them.
Girl Marcia Don't I?
Marcia Yes, I bloody do!
Boy Ralph Of course you don't. Who were you talking to?
Girl Marcia What?
Boy Ralph I heard you. Have you been on the phone?
Marcia Why am I thinking about this now?
Girl Marcia No.
Marcia Stop it.
Girl Marcia I was thinking aloud, that's all.
Boy Ralph Talking to yourself, eh? You know what they say about that.
Marcia I'm not going crazy. Go away.
Boy Ralph What?
Marcia You heard me. (*To Girl Marcia*) And you!
Girl Marcia But I haven't finished taking my ——
Marcia (*firmer*) I said go away! (*She closes her eyes*) Go away!

Both Girl Marcia and Boy Ralph look at each other before they reluctantly leave

The Lights change

Marcia opens her eyes

   Ralph returns

   Comes to something if you can't control your own thoughts.
Ralph (*catching Marcia's last few words*) What?
Marcia (*seeing him*) Nothing.

There's something about Ralph's manner that's different

   What's the matter?
Ralph What do you mean?
Marcia (*crossing to him*) Something wrong?
Ralph No.
Marcia Yes there is, something's wrong.
Ralph There's not ... if you don't count the fact that we should be at our Ruby
   Wedding party and we won't be going because you're leaving me.
Marcia *You* can go. You said you were ——
Ralph I know what I said.
Marcia Why have you changed your mind? I suppose it's to do with
   Malcolm?
Ralph Funnily enough, no. I don't think it will come as a total surprise, but
   it's all to do with you.
Marcia Well, I think you're silly. I think at least one of us should go.
Ralph That is a joke, isn't it? I can't tell with that one.
Marcia There's no reason why *you* shouldn't be there.
Ralph She's serious.
Marcia Absolutely.
Ralph There's no way I'm walking in that place on my own.
Marcia I'm sure you could.
Ralph Yes, of course, I could but I don't *want* to.
Marcia Oh well ... I mean if you don't *want* to, you do want to, do you?
Ralph You'll be sorry for all this one day. One day you're going to wake up
   and you're going to be sorry.

   He leaves the room

A pause

Marcia Is one of us cracking up?

The Lights change and there is a sound effect

   Girl Marcia and Boy Ralph appear

   (*Looking at them both*) Yes ...

Girl Marcia (*sitting on the stool*) I'm not sure who at this stage, but one of us is beginning to show definite signs of dementia. If it turns out to be me I want the pillow over my face.

Boy Ralph Sorry, no can do.

Girl Marcia Why not? I'd do the same for you.

Boy Ralph Would you?

Marcia Yes, I bloody would.

Girl Marcia If it's what you wanted.

Boy Ralph You mean you'd actually be capable of suffocating me?

Marcia You're suffocating *me*.

Girl Marcia I couldn't bear it if your brain scrambled and you didn't know who the hell I was.

Boy Ralph I don't think I know who the hell you are *now*. (*Sitting on the bed*) You'd actually put a pillow over my face and stop me breathing?

Girl Marcia } (*together*) Yes.
Marcia }

Girl Marcia If I thought I'd get away with it. I wouldn't go to prison for you.

Boy Ralph (*smiling*) Forty years and you still surprise me.

Girl Marcia Not everyone can say that.

Marcia Not everyone would want to.

Boy Ralph Probably that's one of the reasons why we've lasted so long ... thank God there's still nooks and crannies we haven't discovered about each other.

Girl Marcia There's not much I don't know about you.

Boy Ralph Are you saying you see through me?

Girl Marcia Transparent as glass.

Boy Ralph What if you're wrong? What if I've got some deep dark secret you don't know about?

Girl Marcia Have you?

Boy Ralph (*smiling*) Maybe.

Marcia (*insisting*) No, I know everything about you.

Boy Ralph What if you're wrong? What if I've got some deep dark secret you don't know about?

Girl Marcia Have you?

Boy Ralph (*smiling*) Maybe.

Marcia Have you?

Boy Ralph (*smiling*) Maybe.

Marcia Have you?

Boy Ralph (*smiling*) Maybe.

Marcia (*shouting*) Ralph! (*She closes her eyes. Calling again*) Ralph!

Suddenly Ralph comes into the room

Girl Marcia and Boy Ralph freeze

How are you getting here so quick? Are you hanging round outside or what?

Ralph I was on the landing ... what do you want?

Marcia (*going to him*) You're keeping something from me.

Ralph What are you talking about?

Marcia I know you are.

Ralph (*after a slight pause*) It isn't anything I want to discuss.

Marcia So I'm right, there *is* something. (*Slight pause*) Look Ralph, if you've got some deep dark secret then I want to know what it is.

Ralph Why? You're leaving. What's it got to do with you?

Marcia (*after a slight pause*) You're right ... why am I getting involved?

Girl Marcia and Boy Ralph leave the room

The Lights change

Ralph I'm ill.

Marcia Ill? What do you mean, ill?

Ralph Ill ... as in out of health.

Marcia What, a bad stomach, you're feeling sick or something?

Ralph It's much more serious than that.

Marcia (*after a slight pause*) Are you kidding me?

Ralph It would be a pretty sick joke if I was.

Marcia thinks about it for a second or two

Marcia No ... no, no, no, no, I'm not falling for it.

Ralph You think I'd lie about something like that?

Marcia Ralph, you'd lie to the Archbishop of Canterbury if you thought it would stop me leaving.

Ralph I didn't tell you so that you wouldn't go. I told you because you asked me.

Marcia (*after a slight pause*) What's the matter with you?

Ralph (*after a slight pause*) It's our old friend. (*Slight pause*) Cancer.

Marcia (*after a slight pause*) What do you mean, "Old friend"?

He doesn't answer

How long have you known?

Ralph Two months.

Marcia (*amazed*) And you've kept it to yourself?

Ralph *You* did.
Marcia I swear to God I didn't know you were ill.
Ralph I mean when *you* had it. You didn't share it with *me*.
Marcia *(after a slight pause)* You knew I had cancer?
Ralph How big a fool do you take me for?
Marcia You never said anything.
Ralph Neither did you. You'd had your treatment *and* had the all-clear by the time *I* found out.
Marcia I tried to tell you.
Ralph But how hard?
Marcia You didn't make it easy for me.
Ralph How hard?

She doesn't answer

Do you know what *I* think? I think you just wanted to cover yourself. I think we could have and *should* have gone through it together ... but that didn't suit you.
Marcia No ... it wasn't like that.
Ralph How was it then?
Marcia I remember I definitely tried to tell you but you were too damned pre-occupied. You should have told me about *you* though.
Ralph How could I turn to you with my problem when you didn't turn to me with yours?
Marcia *(after a slight pause, moving away)* Who else knows?
Ralph Only my doctor.
Marcia The girls?
Ralph No.
Marcia *(after a slight pause)* You said you've known for two months. You've started treatment then?
Ralph No.
Marcia Why not?
Ralph I'm not having any ... there's no point ... there's nothing they can do.
Marcia Are you sure?
Ralph It's not something you get wrong.

A slight pause

Marcia You're taking it very well.
Ralph I've had time to accept it.
Marcia Even so ...
Ralph You don't believe me, do you?
Marcia I have my doubts. You did say you'd do anything to make me stay.

Ralph And my dying would do that? I'm flattered.

Marcia Stop playing games, I need to know if you're dying.

Ralph According to you I was already dead.

Marcia Please ... I have to know.

Ralph No, Marcy ... what you *have* to do is ask yourself what difference it makes ... if any.

Marcia Of course it makes a difference. I can hardly walk out on you if you are.

Ralph Yes you could. Marcia can do anything she likes because Marcia doesn't give a damn for anyone. Anyway, you don't have a choice.

Marcia (*after a slight pause*) What do you mean?

Ralph You don't think I'd let you stay now, do you?

Marcia I thought you'd want me here under any circumstances.

Ralph No ... you flatter yourself.

Marcia But you said ——

Ralph Forget what I said.

Marcia If you're saying the truth I can hardly turn my back on you.

Ralph And if I'm not? (*A slight pause*) I don't want you to stay just because you think I'm dying.

Marcia Is that why you've organized this party tonight? Because you're ill?

Ralph You think I wanted a party because I'm too old for Disney World? I would have wanted a bash whatever my state of health. (*Slight pause*) No, you don't have to get out the policies just yet ... I'm not going to die, Marcia ... I'm as fit as a fiddle, it's our marriage that's sick.

Marcia What? (*Slight pause*) It's all lies then?

Ralph Of course it is ... what's the matter, just a little disappointed?

Marcia You put me through all that ——

Ralph All what? According to you there's nothing between us and hasn't been since God knows when. What are you saying? Are you telling me there's still something there?

Marcia Regardless of what I said, I wouldn't like to see anything happen to you.

Ralph (*after a slight pause*) Do you know that's the nearest you've ever come to telling me you love me.

Marcia I don't love you.

Ralph Of course you do ... Oh, I might not have set any fires raging but you do love me, you're just afraid to admit it, that's all.

Marcia And why would that be?

Ralph Because it scares the shit out of you. (*Slight pause*) I wasn't what you wanted, I knew that. I've known for forty years I've never measured up ... but I've always done my best for you even though it was never good enough.

Marcia No ... it's not your fault. You mustn't blame yourself.

Ralph It's all right, I wasn't.

Marcia almost chokes as she suddenly chuckles. Slight pause

I wanted tonight to be special ... the best night of our lives.

Marcia What can I say?

Ralph You could say "I'll leave tomorrow." You could say, "I can't let all those people down I'll go through it for their sakes." You could even say, "I realize it's a very important night for you, Ralph, and I'll do it just for you."

Marcia The trouble is, even though we've lived together all these years, we think like single people.

Ralph I don't think *I* do ... and deep down, I don't think *you* do either. It's not too late, you know.

Marcia We've been together too long.

Ralph Too long to throw it all away.

Marcia I meant to make changes ... what do they say? Old dogs, new tricks?

Ralph (*after a slight pause, sitting on the stool*) I can't say anything to change your mind then?

Marcia (*after a slight pause*) I'm sorry.

Ralph The shame of it is you have everything ... you just can't appreciate it.

Marcia What's the point of having everything if you've no-one to share it with.

Ralph My thoughts exactly.

Marcia I want something you can't give me, Ralph.

Ralph What makes you think you'll get it from someone else?

Marcia Maybe I won't ... what I can't do is stay put and rot. There has to be something better than this out there for me.

Ralph (*after a pause*) OK ... go and look for it then ... promise me one thing though... if you don't find it, you'll settle for what you had?

Marcia You're telling me I can come back?

Ralph Not that I imagine for a minute you'll want to ... but I'm not going anywhere.

Marcia thinks about it for a split second

Marcia What are you doing?

Ralph What you asked me to do, I'm letting you go ... Just remember though, those that think the grass is greener somewhere else are either selfish, incredibly ungrateful or colour-blind.

Marcia Which do you think I am?

Ralph Probably all three.

Marcia (*joining him at the dressing-table*) I can't leave now, you know that, don't you?

Ralph I've told you, I don't want you to stay just because I'm ill.
Marcia Aha!
Ralph I mean because you *think* I'm ill.
Marcia And I don't want to stay if you're *not*.
Ralph So bugger off then.
Marcia But I don't believe you when you say there's nothing wrong with
   you.
Ralph That's because you don't want to.
Marcia (*getting up and moving* DL) Why?
Ralph Because deep down you don't want to leave.
Marcia So why am I packed?
Ralph That doesn't mean anything. It's just as easy to take the clothes out
   of the suitcase as it is to put them in. To leave you have to actually walk
   through the door ... like this.

He leaves

There is a pause. Marcia is left motionless for a moment

   Girl Marcia and Boy Ralph appear

*There is a sound effect and lighting change, but different to the usual one: the
whole stage is darker and Marcia is now in a blueish spot*

Boy Ralph We have had our moments, haven't we?
Girl Marcia Yes, but that's all they were, Ralph ... moments. In forty years
   they don't add up to much. The trouble is we're not compatible and we
   never were.
Boy Ralph I don't deserve this.
Marcia We both don't.
Boy Ralph I can't imagine my life without you.
Marcia (*shouting*) You're suffocating me, don't you see that?
Girl Marcia Look at me.
Boy Ralph I am looking at you.
Marcia I mean really look at me.
Girl Marcia What do you see?
Boy Ralph We can get through this.
Marcia (*shouting*) Tell me what you see!
Boy Ralph (*shouting back*) I see a silly old woman. (*A pause. Quieter now*)
   I see a silly old woman who can't let go of something and who ought to
   know better.
Girl Marcia Shall I tell you what I see?
Marcia When I look in the mirror ——

Girl Marcia When I look in the mirror I don't see anything ...
Marcia I don't know where I'm going ——
Girl Marcia I only know where I've come from ——
Marcia And what I've left behind.
Girl Marcia Do you have any idea how frightening that is?
Marcia I don't know what it's like to kiss someone ——
Girl Marcia And feel my body fit to explode. I've no idea what it's like to look into someone's eyes ——
Marcia And feel the thrill in my stomach ——
Girl Marcia When it turns over ——
Marcia As if I was on the Big Dipper. No-one has ——
Girl Marcia Ever taken my breath away.
Boy Ralph I wanted tonight to be special ... the best night of our lives.
Girl Marcia What can I say?
Boy Ralph You could say, "I'll leave tomorrow".
Girl Marcia The trouble is, even though we've lived together all these years, we think like single people. We've been together too long.
Marcia Too long to throw it all away. (*A slight pause*) No, wait a minute ... I didn't say that, he did.
Boy Ralph Too long to throw it all away.
Marcia I said about ——
Girl Marcia Old dogs, new tricks? (*Slight pause*) I want something you can't give me, Ralph.
Boy Ralph What makes you think you'll get it from someone else?
Marcia Maybe I won't.
Girl Marcia What I can't do is stay put and rot.
Boy Ralph (*after a slight pause*) OK ... go and look for it then ... promise me one thing though ... if you don't find it, you'll settle for what you had.
Marcia You're telling me I can come back?
Boy Ralph Not that I imagine for a minute you'll want to ... but I'm not going anywhere.

Girl Marcia thinks about it for a split second

Girl Marcia What are you doing?
Boy Ralph What you asked me to do. I'm letting you go.
Marcia (*after a slight pause*) I can't leave you now, you know that, don't you?
Boy Ralph I've told you, I don't want you to stay just because I'm ill.
Girl Marcia Aha!
Boy Ralph I mean because you *think* I'm ill.
Marcia But I don't believe you.
Boy Ralph That's because you don't want to.

Girl Marcia Why?
Marcia Because deep down you don't want to go.

The Lights change (back to the usual one this time)

Boy Ralph I said that.
Marcia I know, but perhaps *I* should have.
Girl Marcia So why am I packed?
Marcia Doesn't mean a thing.
Boy Ralph It's just as easy to take the clothes out of the suitcase as it is to
put them in. To leave you have to actually walk out through the door ... like
this.

Boy Ralph leaves the room

Marcia and Girl Marcia look each other straight in the eye. A slight pause

Marcia (*sighing*) So where do I go from here?
Girl Marcia Seems to me the ball is in my court. (*Slight pause*) Perhaps he's
right you know ... maybe there is a part of me that doesn't want to leave.
Marcia What about the part of me that does?
Girl Marcia I've handled it all these years.
Marcia Meaning I should go on?
Girl Marcia Would it be that impossible?
Marcia You don't know what it's like.
Girl Marcia (*smiling but almost outraged*) You can't say that.
Marcia (*laughing*) No, I can't, of course you do.
Girl Marcia Then there's the illness.

Both Marcias come to sit in the front of the dressing-table

Marcia What am I supposed to make of that?
Girl Marcia He's capable of lying we know.
Marcia But is he on this occasion?
Girl Marcia Your guess is as good as mine.
Marcia Obviously. You know, I was really worried when he told me.
Girl Marcia I didn't show him.
Marcia I didn't want to.
Girl Marcia Perhaps I should have.
Marcia What would be the point of that?
Girl Marcia I don't know, but it wouldn't have done any harm, I know that
much.
Marcia Trouble is, I haven't shown any feeling for so long I've forgotten
how to.

Girl Marcia He's not all to blame then.

Marcia I never said he was ... except for this party thing. That *is* all his doing.

Girl Marcia Even that was good-intentioned.

Marcia I'm not so sure. He knew how I'd react, that's why he kept it quiet.

Girl Marcia He kept it quiet because he wanted to surprise you.

Marcia Whose side are you on?

Girl Marcia I'm just trying to see things from both points of view that's all.

Marcia (*after a slight pause*) I suppose it would have been a nice gesture under normal circumstances.

Girl Marcia I think it was a nice gesture *anyway*.

Marcia Really?

Girl Marcia Come on.

Marcia Well ... maybe.

Girl Marcia And I think you should tell him.

Marcia No way.

Girl Marcia *Someone* has to make the first move.

Marcia Let him do it.

Girl Marcia Under the circumstances ...

Marcia If I say anything encouraging, he'll expect me to go to the damned thing.

Girl Marcia It'll be very embarrassing if I don't turn up.

Marcia I know but I don't care.

Girl Marcia So I keep saying ... don't tell me that deep down there's anything niggling away at me.

Marcia There's not.

Girl Marcia So why am I having this conversation with myself?

Marcia All right, maybe I do wish I could wave a magic wand and make everything right——

Girl Marcia I haven't got to resort to that.

Marcia What should I do then? Give in? Go with the flow?

Girl Marcia From where I'm standing that's what you've been doing anyway.

Marcia From where you're standing is where I'm standing.

Girl Marcia Exactly. Would it be so terrible to carry on?

Marcia God, I sound like Ralph. (*Slight pause*) I'm all mixed up now.

Girl Marcia Don't fight it.

Marcia I can't help it ... I feel like I'm going under for the third time.

Girl Marcia I'm not going to drown ... reach out.

Marcia There's no-one there.

Girl Marcia Of course there is.

Marcia Help me?

Girl Marcia Turn to him.

Marcia Ralph?

Girl Marcia Who else?

Ralph enters the bedroom, followed by Boy Ralph

Ralph You can deny it as much as you like, you definitely talk to yourself.

Marcia and Girl Marcia stand and move R of the dressing-table

Girl Marcia He heard me.
Marcia I was singing.
Boy Ralph That's one of those little white lies she doesn't approve of.
Ralph You're happy then?
Marcia No ... it was a sad song.
Girl Marcia If he'll believe that he'll believe anything.
Boy Ralph She doesn't honestly expect me to believe that?
Ralph I've moved your suitcase from the landing down to the hallway.
Girl Marcia He can't wait to get rid of me.
Boy Ralph What did I tell her that for? She probably thinks I can't wait to
   see the back of her.
Marcia Fine.
Boy Ralph Say something else to her.
Ralph I can always bring it back up if you change your mind.
Boy Ralph That's better.
Girl Marcia Tell him you have.
Boy Ralph Say something else.
Girl Marcia Go on ... tell him.
Ralph I don't suppose you have?
Girl Marcia Tell him.
Marcia No.
Ralph Right.
Girl Marcia What did I say that for?
Marcia Well, I haven't.
Ralph What?
Marcia (*realizing she was thinking aloud*) Oh ... nothing.
Boy Ralph What was that about?
Girl Marcia I must watch I don't do that too often, he thinks I'm half-crazy
   now.
Boy Ralph I reckon she must be cracking up

*Both Marcia and Ralph look at each other. There is a slight pause between
them before they force an embarrassed smile*

Girl Marcia Ask him about his illness again.

Marcia Er ... I was, er ...

Boy Ralph She's hedging. She wants to ask me something.

Girl Marcia How shall I put it?

Marcia Your illness.

Boy Ralph Ah ... we're back to that.

Ralph I'm not ill, I've told you.

Boy Ralph Be very careful what you say here.

Girl Marcia I'd tread very carefully if I were you.

Marcia I'm still not convinced.

Boy Ralph Good.

Ralph What else can I say?

Girl Marcia Tell him to bring the suitcase back upstairs.

Marcia I've been doing a lot of thinking.

Boy Ralph She's not moving out!

Marcia And I'm not moving out.

Boy Ralph (*really excited*) Yes!

Ralph Fine.

Boy Ralph Fine?

Girl Marcia *He's* playing it cool.

Boy Ralph What do I mean, fine?

Ralph I mean good ... I'm glad ... I'm really glad.

Marcia I'm not sure where we go from here.

Boy Ralph She's talking plans.

Ralph One day at a time then, is it?

Marcia OK.

Girl Marcia Show a bit of enthusiasm.

Marcia One day at a time is fine by me.

Ralph It's how we started out, after all.

Marcia I can't argue with that.

Boy Ralph Ask her about the party.

Ralph No.

Marcia What?

Ralph God, *I'm* doing it now.

Marcia What?

Ralph Nothing.

Girl Marcia (*after a slight pause*) What am I going to do about the party?

Ralph (*moving to the champagne*) There's some champagne left. Shall we finish it off? (*He pours*)

Marcia moves in front of the dressing-table

Boy Ralph I don't want to push it ... but how can I get her to the party?

Girl Marcia (*moving behind the stool*) I hope to God I'm doing the right thing.

Ralph (*handing her a glass*) Cheers. (*He drinks*)

   Boy Ralph and Girl Marcia leave the room

The Lights change

Ralph I've forgotten to mention your surprise present.
Marcia I don't like surprises.
Ralph You'll like this.
Marcia What is it?
Ralph It's a Caribbean cruise.
Marcia Really?
Ralph For four?
Marcia We're taking the girls? (*She sips her champagne*)
Ralph No, Malcolm and Eileen.

Marcia almost chokes

   Are you all right?
Marcia Are you serious?
Ralph Are you OK? I was only kidding.
Marcia I'm fine.
Ralph (*after a slight pause*) You know, for a minute there ... I thought I took your breath away.

There is a moment between them. Suddenly the phone rings

   (*Answering it*) Hallo? (*A slight pause*) Yes, hang on. (*To Marcia*) It's Judith this time. She wants a word.

He offers her the receiver but she pauses before accepting it

Marcia (*eventually, into the phone*) Hallo, Jude? ... Yes ... everything's fine.

Ralph sips his champagne as the Lights begin to fade, accompanied by a sound effect

CURTAIN

FURNITURE AND PROPERTY LIST

ACT I

On stage: Double bed. *On it*: pillows, bedclothes
Two wardrobes. *In* **Marcia's**: suitcase, items of clothing including
four dresses, one of very shiny material. *In* **Ralph's**: ties on a rack
Bedside cabinets. *On one*: telephone. *In one*: birthday card
Dressing-table. *On it*: make-up. *In drawer*: underwear, etc.
Stool
Large bedroom chair
Exercise bike
Pair of shoes for **Marcia**
Ali-baba basket
Low table. *On it*: stereo

Off stage: Handbag (**Girl Marcia**)
Bottle of champagne, two glasses (**Ralph**)
Two birthday cards in envelopes (**Girl Marcia**)
Two glasses of whisky (**Boy Ralph**)
Two glasses of whisky (**Ralph**)

Personal: **Girl Marcia**: corsage
Boy Ralph: bottle of cologne in Boots' bag in jacket pocket
Ralph: wrist-watch

ACT II

On stage: As Act I

Off stage: Shoes, tail-coat, cravat, corsage (**Boy Ralph**)
Box of paper hankies (**Ralph**)

LIGHTING PLOT

Property fittings required: nil
Interior. The same scene throughout

ACT I

To open: General interior lighting

Cue 1	**Girl Marcia** enters *Change to bluish wash*	(Page 1)
Cue 2	**Boy Ralph** and **Girl Marcia** exit *Revert to general interior lighting*	(Page 6)
Cue 3	**Girl Marcia** appears *Change to bluish wash*	(Page 11)
Cue 4	**Girl Marcia** walks off into the bathroom *Revert to general interior lighting*	(Page 13)
Cue 5	**Boy Ralph** comes in through the door *Change to bluish wash*	(Page 18)
Cue 6	**Girl Marcia** leaves with the jacket *Revert to general interior lighting*	(Page 21)
Cue 7	**Boy Ralph** comes out of the bathroom *Change to bluish wash*	(Page 21)
Cue 8	**Boy Ralph** and **Girl Marcia** leave *Revert to general interior lighting*	(Page 23)
Cue 9	**Girl Marcia** comes out of the bathroom *Change to bluish wash*	(Page 27)
Cue 10	**Boy Ralph** goes into the bathroom *Revert to general interior lighting*	(Page 31)
Cue 11	Telephone ringing increases in volume *Fade to black-out*	(Page 34)

Lighting Plot   67

ACT II

To open: General interior lighting

Cue 12   **Girl Marcia** comes into the room   (Page 35)
             Change to bluish wash

Cue 13   **Boy Ralph** gets up and leaves the room   (Page 37)
             Revert to general interior lighting

Cue 14   **Girl Marcia** comes in   (Page 39)
             Change to bluish wash

Cue 15   **Girl Marcia** leaves and **Boy Ralph** follows her   (Page 43)
             Revert to general interior lighting

Cue 16   **Marcia** turns back into the room   (Page 50)
             Change to bluish wash

Cue 17   **Girl Marcia** and **Boy Ralph** reluctantly leave   (Page 51)
             Revert to general interior lighting

Cue 18   **Marcia**: " ... cracking up?"   (Page 52)
             Change to bluish wash

Cue 19   **Girl Marcia** and **Boy Ralph** leave   (Page 54)
             Revert to general interior lighting

Cue 20   **Girl Marcia** and **Boy Ralph** appear   (Page 58)
             Dim lighting; bring up blue spot on **Marcia**

Cue 21   **Marcia**: " ... you don't want to go."   (Page 60)
             Increase lighting, cut blue spot

Cue 22   **Boy Ralph** and **Girl Marcia** leave the room   (Page 64)
             Revert to general interior lighting

Cue 23   **Ralph** sips his champagne   (Page 64)
             Fade to black-out

EFFECTS PLOT

A licence issued by Samuel French Ltd to perform this play does not include permission to use the Incidental music specified in this copy. Where the place of performance is already licensed by the PERFORMING RIGHT SOCIETY a return of the music used must be made to them. If the place of performance is not so licensed then application should be made to the Performing Right Society, 29 Berners Street, London W1.

A separate and additional licence from PHONOGRAPHIC PERFORMANCES LTD, Ganton House, Ganton Street, London W1 is needed whenever commercial recordings are used.

ACT I

Cue 1	To open *Music transfers from front of house to stereo*	(Page 1)
Cue 2	**Marcia** switches off the stereo *Cut music*	(Page 1)
Cue 3	**Girl Marcia** enters *Sound effect*	(Page 2)
Cue 4	**Boy Ralph** appears *Sound effect*	(Page 2)
Cue 5	**Girl Marcia** appears *Sound effect*	(Page 11)
Cue 6	**Boy Ralph** comes in *Sound effect*	(Page 12)
Cue 7	**Boy Ralph** comes in through the door *Sound effect*	(Page 18)
Cue 8	**Girl Marcia** comes in *Sound effect*	(Page 20)
Cue 9	**Boy Ralph** comes out of the bathroom *Sound effect*	(Page 21)

ACT II

Cue 25   **Ralph**: " ... your breath away." Slight pause   (Page 64)
            Telephone

Cue 26   **Ralph** sips his champagne   (Page 64)
            Sound effect